7 SIMPLE STEPS TO
RECOVERY

Find Out How to Get a Grip on Addiction and Find Freedom

7 SIMPLE STEPS TO

RECOVERY

REV. Charles F. Plauché
OVER 25 YEARS OF ADDICTION RECOVERY EXPERIENCE

Printed in the United States of America.
Library of Congress Control Number: 2020920638
ISBN: 978-1-73511-122-3

*This book is dedicated to all those who are still suffering
and the families who love them.*

CONTENTS

INTRODUCTION:

The Reality of Addiction

As Americans, we come across stories of addiction all the time. It is talked about on the news, in our schools, and throughout political campaigns. Addiction has become a common plot point in our entertainment, whether on television, in books, or in films. We have been trained to spot the behavior, to recognize the tropes, and to anticipate the often-tragic outcome. We wring our hands and shake our heads—we all know addiction is awful.

What is less talked about in American culture is *recovery from addiction*. Aside from some popularized images of AA meetings and the vague concept of 12 Step programs, what happens in recovery has remained somewhat of a mystery for most people. There is a notion that there is no such *thing* as real recovery. A common refrain tells addicts and their families that once you're addicted, you're an addict for life, and this self-defeating idea can often do more harm than good.

If you're reading this book, chances are you're either an addict yourself, or you know and love one. You already know the simple,

1

brutal reality of addiction from firsthand experience—it destroys lives, futures, and families. Now I am here to tell you that despite what you may have heard, despite how dark things seem right now, there is hope. There can be life after addiction. As the executive director of Haven House Addiction Recovery, a nonprofit organization for men in recovery, and as a former addict myself, I know that recovery is possible, and I'm going to explain how.

Maybe you've picked up this book because you are sick of struggling with the substance that has become the center of your life. Maybe you're exhausted and ready for the insanity to stop but can't find the exit. You feel ready for your legal problems to go away, or you want to be able to find and keep a job. You're ready to stop fighting with your spouse or to stop feeling physically ill. You know it's time to stop the lying, the manipulation, the self-loathing. You're ready to rid yourself of the anger that has been at the center of your life for as long as you have been addicted.

But how? Knowing you're ready to stop and knowing *how* to stop are two very different things. Maybe you're not sure you can do it. Maybe you've tried before and have not been successful. You're worried that if you try again and fail, you risk disappointing everyone, most of all yourself. After all, why would this time be any different? During my years at Haven House, I have learned this: *most people* think that it's impossible for them at first. Even when they are ready to be done with the suffering, most people think, "The things I have done in the name of my addiction are too terrible. There's no coming back."

However, my decades at Haven House have also confirmed that *anyone* can move past a life of addiction. With a strong commitment to creating a new life for yourself, there is nothing you can't come back from. I have seen it work for so many people, people who could never have imagined a different way of living. And it all begins the first moment you think, "I'm ready."

However, the fact that everyone *can* recover does not mean that everyone *will* recover. The process might be simple, but it is not easy. It involves hard work, commitment, and self-reflection. Those things can be difficult, especially for addicts. You've got to ask yourself, *What do I have to lose?* You know that something has to change, so why not take the chance on a better life? As I always say to our new residents, "Give us ninety days to try. If it doesn't work for you in ninety days, we'll gladly refund your misery."

Maybe you're hesitant because of things you've heard, either through previous programs or pop-culture depictions of recovery. Are you intimidated by the idea of handing yourself over to a higher power, or nervous about making amends at some point? Maybe you've been given the impression that you're going to have to be perfect every moment of every day.

I'm here to help you prepare for the inevitabilities and disavow you of any wrongheaded ideas you may have picked up along the way. This book will help you understand what to expect throughout recovery, step by step. It is intended to remove the mystery and explain in simple terms what lies ahead.

Stopping Is Just the Start

The process of recovery is much more complicated than just ceasing the use of drugs or alcohol—that is just the outward result. Recovery is about developing a lifestyle and habits that will allow the abstention to continue and the desire to become less and less of a burden every day.

Sometimes I compare recovery to learning to play guitar. Nobody picks up a guitar and plays like Stevie Ray Vaughan the very first time. When you are learning, you play slowly; you fumble around. You have to get calluses on your fingers, learn chords, develop muscle memory. It's a step-by-step process of practice and repetition, until it finally becomes second nature. Eventually, being a musician is no longer something you do—it is who you are. It's how you live.

Being substance-free is the same. It has to become who we *are*, rather than something we *do*. Throughout this book, I will refer to the steps as being part of a "program." This is shorthand for the whole process, and you will hear this word a lot, both from me and from other recovery groups. But I want you to keep in mind that in some ways, "program" is a poor description of the transformative experience we are encouraging. Unlike some other recovery programs, at Haven House, sobriety becomes the way you *live*, not a program that you engage in during designated hours of the day. You are learning a whole new way of life, and for most people, nothing short of that will give you long-lasting results.

This was true for me. When my "I'm ready" moment came, I had been drinking heavily every day, and I had never been so low. I had nothing to hold onto in my life—I had driven away family and friends; I was wasting my potential. I was able to stay sober long enough to go to work during the day, but by the late afternoon, I started drinking, and I wouldn't stop until I passed out. I was miserable and lonely—"Alone in a crowded room" is how I used to describe the feeling.

Eventually, I realized I could not go on that way. Desperate for change but not sure what to do, I called my father for advice.

"Get on a plane and come back home," he said.

I had been living out of state and had not expected this response. "What about all my stuff? What about my car?"

"Just pick up what you can carry," he said. "We can get more stuff, Son. You just get on the plane and come home."

My dad was a wise man. He taught me I could always get more physical belongings, but I did not have an endless number of opportunities to get my life back on track. Eventually my health and luck would run out, and I needed to seize this moment of clarity, no matter the cost.

So, in a rare moment of good decision-making, I did what my father told me to do: I left my vehicle and everything I owned behind, and I flew home. I was in treatment the next day.

I would like to tell you it wasn't hard, or that I was successful right away. But I can't tell you that, and you should not expect that for yourself either. I had to try several different places before it "took," which is to say, I had to try a few places before I was *really* ready. You'll often hear an addict say, "That place just didn't work for me." I said it a few times myself. The truth is, the places worked fine. *I* wouldn't work for *them*. It took me a while to truly be ready for change.

> **I would like to tell you it wasn't hard, or that I was successful right away. But I can't tell you that, and you should not expect that for yourself either.**

Whenever we bring people in to our program, we begin by asking, "Do you know that you have a problem and you need help? Good. That's all we want. You can even be mad as hell about it, but you have to know."

You know all those concerns you have, about the higher power, or making amends, or other things you saw on TV? Put them away for now. On day one, all we are asking you to say is, "I know this is an issue, and it's time to deal with it." We don't ask you to own the whole problem right away. We don't ask you to fully embrace a religion or even religiosity. We don't need you to come to terms with the depth or breadth of your actions. On day one, all you need to do is say, "I'm ready."

The Bible tells us, "Don't put a stumbling block or hindrance in the way of a brother," and at Haven House, what we are trying to do is clear the path. You're standing on the beginning of the path, and we will make sure nothing will impede the way to a new life but you.

It's Up to You

Addiction doesn't care who you are, who your parents are, where you went to school, what your education level is, or how much money you have or don't have. It does not discriminate against any skin color, religion, or geographical location. There is no demographic that is "safe" from addiction—it crosses all boundaries and touches all walks of life. It's one of the things about drug addiction that is so scary. No one is safe. There is no "typical addict."

> **It's one of the things about drug addiction that is so scary. No one is safe. There is no "typical addict."**

Despite this, addicts do share some commonalities. For one thing, if you scratch the surface of an addict, you'll usually find a family history of addiction. It might not have been opioid addiction, but dear old Mom may have liked Valium a bit too much, or Grandma Sally was a drinker, or Uncle Jack had a gambling problem … and so on and so forth. Addiction runs in families, and that means some of us might be genetically or socially predisposed to be at risk.

There are also emotional parallels between addicts. I've spoken to thousands of addicts throughout my life, and I've been one. Most of us admit to having similar insecurities: "I never felt like I fit in" or "Somehow I just didn't belong." When we outsiders take our first drink or snort our first line, all of a sudden, everything changes. We are a little bolder, a little funnier, a little more capable of fitting in with the crowd. Once that line has been crossed, we often find out we're predisposed, and then we can't stop.

Occasionally I meet someone who never seemed to have an issue but found themselves hooked on medication after a surgery or an accident. It does happen, but for the most part, it's the combination of nurture and nature that leads to addiction.

And just as addicts have similarities, the addictions themselves—as wide and varied as they are—do too. Today, opioid dependence is a growing epidemic in the United States, and there are definitely aspects to this particular form of addition that are unique. Unlike alcohol, which can be purchased legally by adults, from the first moment you are abusing opioids, you are breaking the law. This only gets worse as you fall further and further into the addiction and have to sacrifice your morals, dignity, and reputation to get more drugs.

The physical effects of opioids are also swift—and more dire. The damage on your organs, your brain function, and your outward appearance will occur in a much shorter time and will be harder to reverse. This, in combination with the immediate legal trouble, makes opioid addiction seem like a new, insurmountable problem.

But when you get down to basics, almost all addicts are the same. The causes, the root problems, the lying and manipulative behaviors—they all come with every addiction, no matter what the substance. The recovery is the same as well, and this book is a resource to understanding the steps you must take to get there, whether you are drinking alcohol, sniffing glue, or shooting meth.

I'm telling you this in the hopes that it will make you feel less alone. There are very few addiction origin stories I have not encountered in some form or another throughout my years, and like I said, anyone can recover if they are ready and willing.

Just as no one can make you take a drink or swallow a pill, no one can make you stop. People can ask you stop, and they probably have—repeatedly. But the real change won't happen until you yourself are ready. No one else can control your recovery. It's what we call an "inside job."

As we often say, "The bad news is that it's up to you. The good news is, it's up to you." Buying this book is a good sign that you have come to an important crossroad and are finally ready to make a meaningful change. You are ready to write your own story, to make sure this tale of addiction has a happy ending.

So, welcome. I am glad we can go on this journey together.

STEP 1:

I Am Ready to Admit That
I Am the Problem, and
I Can't Do It Alone

The First Step is deceptively simple. It is the moment when an addict admits that he is, in fact, part of the problem, and needs help to change his behavior.

That's it. "I admit that I am the problem, and I can't do it alone."

About thirteen words, and you've completed the First Step.

However, as simple as it sounds, it is far from easy. When an addict begins using drugs, she suddenly feels like she fits in for the first time in her life, and nothing will get in her way. It doesn't matter that she feels lousy when she's coming down, or that she has to break the law or put herself in danger to get her next fix. It doesn't matter when she loses her job, her health, and her money. She doesn't care if her family or friends tell her she's out of control and needs help. She will justify, defend, and contort the situation to get what she wants.

Addicts are world-class manipulators, and they will tell you that they are just victims of circumstance, that *nothing* is their fault, or that they are not that different from everyone else, until they are blue in the face. "What is the big deal if I do a little cocaine? Everyone does this once in a while." Or "If you weren't on my case so much, I wouldn't need a drink to calm down!"

The longer an addict uses, the more entrenched in the lifestyle they become, and the further down the hole of lies and manipulation they have to travel. Ultimately, a whole house of cards is built on the premise that there is nothing wrong, there is no problem, and if you think they have a problem, then you're the one with the problem. One moment of real ownership, of true admission, and the whole thing will come crashing down.

Addicts are also notoriously self-absorbed—convinced that they have all the answers and are the center of the universe. An addict has it all worked out, has figured it out from top to bottom, and they don't need you sticking your nose into something you know nothing about. If you try to tell an addict they have a problem, they will find a way to turn it back on you. "Oh, I'm the one with a problem? How many glasses of wine do *you* have with dinner?"

Sound familiar? Have you heard these things, or maybe even said them yourself? Have you been lying to everyone, including the face in the mirror, about what's really going on? Are you convinced you can't let anyone in, lest they find out the truth about you? Do you feel miserable, sick, and ready to put an end to the suffering?

Welcome to Step 1. *This is the moment when you have to admit, "There's an actual problem here. I can't continue this way."*

Sometimes there is an inciting incident. You've wrecked your car again, or you've ruined another family gathering. Maybe you've finally lost the job you've been barely hanging on to, or your long-suffering spouse is packing up to leave. For some people, their life will continue on a downward

This is the moment when you have to admit, "There's an actual problem here. I can't continue this way."

spiral until finally they have nothing and no one. Their whole life is empty. They are alone in an empty house. They are sitting in jail. They are homeless. It can sometimes take a dramatic catalyst to make someone open her eyes, to think, "There's a common denominator to all these disasters, and it's me. Maybe I really *am* part of the problem."

Sometimes there is no definitive event. A series of terrible choices and behaviors can draw a man into a life of misery until he wakes up one day and decides he just can't go on like this. That's how it happened for me. I was still "functioning" on some level, but I was despondent, lonely—I'd had enough. All of a sudden I just came to the realization, "Maybe I have something to do with this problem. Maybe it's not everyone else's fault."

This may sound like a subtle shift, but for a person who struggles with addiction, this is a monumental adjustment. As I mentioned, addicts are skilled at blaming everyone else for their problems. "My boss has always had it in for me" or "My parents are never satisfied no matter what I do, so why bother?" Assuming *any* of the blame means there is a crack in the veneer, a weakness in the barrier to change.

It is a small shift in thought, but it's that shift that can make all the difference.

The Bible tells us the story of the prodigal son, who, unlike his responsible older brother, squandered away his wealth and was drawn into an irresponsible, sinful life. In the Bible, when he has had enough of his exhausting lifestyle, it says, "He finally came to himself." He came back to who he was really supposed to be, saw that his life was not working, and headed home to his father.

Like the prodigal son, *reaching the First Step is coming back to ourselves*. Not only do we remember who we really are—the person our addiction and lies stole from us and the people who love us—but we also come to see the truth: that we, ourselves, are at the center of this problem.

Today Is What Matters

It's a rare person who comes to this realization early in their addiction, but it does happen. Every once in a while, there is someone who recognizes the problem at the first sign of trouble and gets help right away. However, if you are like most addicts, you are caught in a long, repetitive spiral that takes you around and around, each time pulling you deeper down. People become accustomed to remarkable things over time, which is how a married father can end up in a crack den or a promising college student can end up living on the street. You might be using drugs for ten, twenty, even thirty years until, like the prodigal son, you "come back to yourself" and own your role in the charade.

Getting to the point where you'll admit that you share some culpability in the matter can take forever. The truth is, some people never get there, because their ego and pride will not let them take responsibility. They've cultivated a habit of blaming everyone else. If they admit their own role, it means their whole life is a lie.

You know the expression "Rome wasn't built in a day"? *Well, years or decades of behavior and thought patterns can't be undone in one step either.* Addicts develop defense mechanisms; these are the behaviors that allow them to continue their addiction despite the disastrous effect it has on their health, life, and relationships. The wall an addict builds to protect himself from the truth, which allows him to blame everyone else and deny responsibility—that cannot be torn down in a day. And the truth is, you don't want it to come down all at once, because that would also be calamitous.

Facing what you've done to the people around you and what you have done to yourself is a process—hence the multiple steps. Admitting to everything all at once, opening that door and letting all that guilt and shame crash in on you in an instant—that could literally kill a person. For a lot of addicts, their defense mechanisms are keeping them alive.

You have to take down the wall slowly, bit by bit, one step at a time. That's why Step 1 is admitting you are *part* of the problem, not owning everything you have done and every decision you have made. That is coming farther down the road. For now, let's just unlock the door and open it a crack. It's still further than a lot of addicts will ever get in their lifetime.

The Inside Job

I've said it before, but it bears repeating; there is nothing that I (or anyone else, for that matter) can say or do to make you become an addict. Understanding this is a powerful part of the First Step. You will often hear addicts say, "It was my brother who got me hooked" or "I had this traumatic event, and that's what got me started." But the truth is, short of holding you down, opening your mouth, and pouring the booze in, nobody can make you drink. Aside from holding you down, tying your arm, and pushing a needle in your vein, no one can make you shoot up either. All of the things that you've done, you've done to and by yourself.

By the same accord, there is nothing I can say or do to make you *quit* using drugs or drinking either. I'm sorry; I am sure life would be much easier if someone could wave a magic wand in your direction and set things right, but that is just not how it works.

This is the reason it is so important that a person come willingly, out of their own desire to get better. No mom, dad, wife, or child can make you do this. Family can be part of your reason to want to change, part of your inspiration to stick with it, a huge part of your goals for sobriety, but they simply cannot give you the will to save your own life. That has to come from within.

At the same time, trying to "trick" or "cajole" an addict into recovery won't work either. We see it all the time at Haven House. We'll get a call from a parent who says, "We've told him he's just coming there for thirty days, so play along. We'll have the whole month to convince him to stay there a year."

That's a deal breaker for us and a major red flag. Anyone who walks through our doors needs to know what he's doing, where he's going, how long it'll be, and what we expect from him throughout.

"But he won't come if he thinks it's more than thirty days," they'll tell us.

"Then he's not ready to admit he is part of the problem," we say. "And guess what? You treating him like a child is not helping him."

We don't give out lollipops for good behavior. Our residents come here with their eyes open and ready to work hard, because they understand they are part of the problem and they can't change things on their own. They haven't been manipulated by anyone through promises and lies.

I've never talked anyone into treatment. I might be able to, for a day or two. But unless they have that internal, burning desire, it's never going to work. If you have to persuade someone into treatment, you're going to be talking them into it again tomorrow, and the next day, and then the day after that, and so on.

Many places are like Haven House—they are clear about the First Step and the inside job. However, other places are less scrupulous, and the convincing and bargaining does happen in order to get addicts to enroll. People who are persuaded into a recovery center will never really commit to the change in their hearts. Addicts might do well while they're in residence because they are being given the structure and the will. But what do you think is the first thing they will do when they are free to walk out the doors? They will go and get high. If there's nobody to talk them into their sobriety and they haven't really done any of the work to change their life, there will be nothing to stop them when temptation rears its ugly head.

I don't mean to imply that an addict won't need moral, emotional and spiritual support. They will need all of that, in excess. An addict will need guidance and advice, a family member or friend who will say, "Let's go talk to a professional" or "Let's go to a meeting." We all need someone to remind us why we're doing it, remind us what the future can hold, and affirm that it will be difficult but worth it. That's invaluable and necessary, but that's different from trying to force somebody. External pressure from any source is not going to motivate real change.

Sometimes we'll have someone come into the program because he is trying to avoid consequences. For example, we had someone who started probation and had nine months left when he started at Haven House. He did really well for exactly nine months, but the moment the probation ran out, he started to cause all kinds of problems. He'd found a way to stay out of trouble while on probation—by living in our program and letting our rules do his work for him. Once he was in the clear, he immediately tried (and succeeded) to get us to kick him out.

It's not an uncommon occurrence. If a person is only trying to beat the system, then as soon as the court looks away, or a wife says, "OK, you can come home now," he's gone, and any good work he might have done is lost.

That is not to say that it's wrong to want to go to treatment and get sober because you're facing some legal problems—that's fine. That means you're *sane*. Not wanting to go to jail, not wanting to pay fines, not wanting to sacrifice your life on the altar of addiction—that means some part of you is thinking straight, and it's a place to start. But acknowledging that you are at least partly responsible, that your impending legal issues are because of *your* behavior, that is essential to any future success.

There Is No Middle Ground

Sometimes you will hear an addict say, "OK, I'm ready for change, but I don't think I need to quit *completely*." An alcoholic might promise to cut down to two beers a night. A crack addict will pledge to only smoke on the weekends.

I can't begin to tell you how often an addict thinks that switching from one substance to another is a sign of progress. They trade in their bourbon for beer, or their hard drugs for pot. People will come to us and say:

"This isn't my first time getting sober, you know. Once I was sober for three years!"

"No kidding. How did you do that?"

"I smoked pot every day."

I've got news for any aspiring "minimizers"—*there is no such thing as a safe number of drugs or amount of alcohol for a person with substance addiction.* If you recognize that a substance has led to huge financial, emotional, and spiritual difficulties in your life, but you still want to keep using "in moderation," you may have a bigger problem than you think. When I hit my hand with a hammer, it hurts. I have control over the hammer, so when that happens, I put it down. I don't see the damage and say, "Well, I'm just going to hit two out of my five fingers on my left hand today."

Why do you need to keep doing it? Because you can't stop. And that is the real problem. You.

This is frustrating and painful realization for many people. "Why are others able to drink or smoke pot in moderation, but I can't?" There is no easy answer. Addiction is a product of both environment and genetics, but in the end, the "why" is unimportant. What matters is the true understanding that you are not like most other people when it comes to substances. You can't just take it or leave it.

In order to manage this problem, you're going to need some support. If you are a heroin addict who has ruined her life, relationships, and reputation, and your best idea is to smoke pot on the weekends, it's time to consider that you don't have access to the best solutions on your own. It's time to get help.

Half-hearted attempts at "change" are a sign that a person is not yet ready to admit they are part of the problem. We often see these warning signs when we are doing intake interviews for our program. Sometimes, it only takes a phone call.

"All right, tell me about what's going on."

"Well, my mom thought it would be a good idea for me to call you."

"Why would she think that?"

"Well, I don't know. Occasionally I'll go out with my buddies and get a little high or something, but it's no big deal."

If there's hesitation or minimizing during the first call, then we know an addict is probably just not ready to admit they need help. Or if they are continuing to make excuses or spin wild tales, then they're still looking for places to place the blame and have not yet recognized that they are at the center of the problem.

"I've heard you've been in some trouble with the law."

"Yeah, if that stupid cop hadn't pulled me over, none of this would have happened."

But the cop pulled you over because you were drunk and weaving back and forth. You were the one drunk! That was the choice you made.

Other people are better at misdirection, and it's not until they are already in the program that it becomes clear their hearts aren't in it. After all, addicts do possess the skill for weaving a web of lies. In the end, the person who suffers the most from an addict's lies is the addict himself. You're not doing us any favors coming into our program without your whole heart, and you're not going to get through recovery and see lasting change if you keep lying to yourself and everyone around you.

How Is This Different from the 12 Steps?

In the traditional 12-Step program, the First Step is admitting that you are powerless over a substance and that your life has become unmanageable. While the essence and spirit of the step remains the same, we have made adjustments for several important reasons.

We don't want to force anybody out by the language we use. For one thing, many people with substance issues do not think of themselves as powerless or find their lives unmanageable. "I go to work every day; I've got a car and a roof over my head. My life is not that unmanageable, so maybe things aren't so bad."

In popular culture, Step 1 is usually depicted as immediately following the ubiquitous "rock bottom." You know what I'm talking about: a person is homeless, living on the street; they've sold all of their belongings, maybe even their body, just to get more drugs. They've lost their teeth, or their skin is ruined, or they have track marks all over their arms and in between their toes. Maybe they've killed someone with their vehicle or robbed their grandmother blind in order to pay for their next fix.

These things definitely happen, and I've seen them all in my line of work. But that doesn't mean they are a *prerequisite* to recovery. People don't have to wait until everything is gone to make a change. You can avoid a rock bottom and get help before these things happen. The truth is, there is no "bottom." Things can always get worse. There is no point in waiting for things to get worse before you look for help. If you can admit to being part of the problem earlier in the process, you can save yourself some of the pain and suffering that comes with years of drug or alcohol abuse.

Also, some people need to retain some semblance of power in order to feel like they have a chance to beat this. I personally never responded to the idea of powerlessness. I'm a go-getter type, and I wanted to believe that I could be a part of the solution. That doesn't mean I am not part of the problem—quite the opposite. If I am at the center of the problem, then *only I* can be the solution to that problem, and that idea didn't feel like powerlessness to me. If you are not the problem, there is no solution!

If I am at the center of the problem, then only I can be the solution to that problem, and that idea didn't feel like powerlessness to me. If you are not the problem, there is no solution!

Remember, every journey begins with the First Step. In this case, that bit of wisdom is both figurative and literal. As short as the actual step may be, it can feel like a mountain to some of us, and there is a lot of work that goes into understanding that you are part of the problem, and you can't do it alone.

As you begin this difficult, important, transformative process, here are some things to keep in mind:

- Step 1 is deceptively simple—it might be thirteen words, but for some people, it takes a lifetime to say them.

- Addicts are trained to blame everyone else for their problems. It might seem like a subtle change, but taking responsibility for part of the problem is actually a seismic shift.

- Whether or not there was an event that led to this step, any crack in the wall of denial is a good first sign.

- Like the prodigal son, you must "come to yourself."

- Rome wasn't built (or unbuilt) in a day. Facing what you've done to the people around you, and what you have done to yourself, is a process—hence the multiple steps.

- It's an inside job—no one can be talked into sobriety. Just as no one can make you use drugs, no one can make you quit.

It has to be a decision you come to yourself, or you'll never stick with it.

- Everyone needs support, guidance, and advice, but no one can do the work for you.

- You're not like other people—recreational drug use is not possible. If drugs and alcohol have ruined your life, and you still can't swear them off completely, you might have a bigger problem than you think.

- Half-hearted is half a heart too short—you can't fake your way into a program. It's clear when someone is not yet ready to accept responsibility. Make sure you're being honest with yourself.

- You don't have to hit rock bottom. You can make a change in your life today, without waiting one more minute.

- If you are at the center of the problem, then only you can be the solution to that problem.

CHANGE

STEP 2:

I Am Ready for Change in My Life

So now you've admitted that you are part of the problem, and you cannot handle it alone. But what are you going to do about it? How can you begin to address the disaster your life has become? Accepting ownership of the *problem* is one thing, but accepting ownership of the *change* necessary to deal with the problem is something else. Committing to change is what Step 2 is all about.

Committing to change is harder than it sounds. An addict can face many terrifying things throughout their "career," but nothing is scarier than change. I have done outreach in all kinds of terrible, sad, and dangerous places where people are struggling. For years I have fed and clothed the homeless and while doing so handed my card out to many people living under bridges and in the woods. And do you know how many of them ended up calling me to ask for help? Zero. Sometimes people are afraid of the unknown and would rather live under a bridge, struggle to find food, battle the elements, and live in filth, than come inside and confront addition.

For those people, change is the true threat. They are used to the weather, and the illness, and the violence that comes with a life on the streets. If they come inside, clean themselves up, and really face a mirror, they might have to face what they've become and what they need to do to fix the problem.

Even once you've begun to accept the fact that you are at the center of the problem, it's not a given that you can commit to change. We lose a lot of people at Step 2, because they don't fully understand what they've agreed to do. Some people come in to the program thinking they will learn how to change everyone else and that we're going to help them.

"Listen, I know I do drugs, but at the heart of it, my wife is wrong, my dad is wrong, and my boss is wrong. Let me explain it to you, and then after you agree, maybe you can help me straighten them out, talk to them, or teach me how to handle them. Because I might be part of it, but if I could just get them to go along, everything would be fine."

Of course, it's entirely possible that there *are* people who contribute to the circumstances surrounding your addiction. I have seen it all: codependent spouses, enabling bosses, triggering siblings, and addiction-buddy parents—none of whom are helping the situation.

Ultimately, these people *do* need to change also. When there is an addict in the family, chances are, the whole family is sick.

But as I said in chapter 1, no one can force you to abuse substances. At the core of your addiction is always you. *Part of being ready to change your life is accepting that you can't control anyone else.* It's time to clean up your side of the street. And you might not be able to change anyone else's behavior, but if you are the center

Part of being ready to change your life is accepting that you can't control anyone else.

of the problem, you are also the center of the solution.

A Commitment You Will Return to Again and Again

It's important to recognize that Step 2 involves committing yourself to making a change—but *it does not mean you will have to change your whole life in a day.* There is a popular depiction of addiction that we have all come to know. It involves making amends, doing good works, going to meetings, living life on the straight and narrow. All of that is important and will come later down the road. Step 2 is about laying the groundwork, mentally preparing for the fact that your life is going to have to change. It means making a commitment to your emotional, physical, and spiritual health.

I can't stress enough how important it is to make this commitment, because there will come many moments throughout the process when it is challenged. When you start down this path, you begin to own the fact that everything you've said and done since the day you started getting drunk and high has been a lie. The excuses, the reasoning, the blaming, the lost jobs, the failed relationships, the estranged family members—all of it is the result of your actions and lies.

Once you start facing this reality, there will be many tough days. There will be many times you want to look us in the eye and say, "It's not my fault; I didn't do it." And we're going to look you right back and say, "It is, and you did." You're not with your mom and dad and girlfriend anymore. They might have let you walk away, or given you a hug, or said, "All is forgiven" without making you work for it. But not us. We are going to tell it like it is. You can't lie to us, because we've been there ourselves, and we know all the tricks. You're going to start feeling a lot of pressure.

That pressure is important. It can keep you going and keep you focused. But it is also dangerous for a person who struggles with addiction—we don't tend to have good track records with pressure. Very often pressure is a trigger or an excuse to indulge in our addiction. We often use drugs to escape that pressure, and since people probably expect us to buckle under said pressure anyway, we think that we might as well go ahead and let everyone down.

With every step of recovery, with every breakthrough and improvement, the pressure will continue to mount. The better you are doing, the higher the stakes will become, and the more and more you will have to lose. As time goes on, you will also have to face more reality—acknowledge more of what you have done and own more of what you will have to do to change your life.

Things will get very tough, and at times you will be tempted to quit. That is when you will remember Step 2 and your commitment to changing your life. You will remember the work you did, the preparations you made, and the reasons you have for changing. Without that touchstone, you can get fed up, frustrated, and lost in individual actions, and you can lose track of the bigger picture of intention.

If you are like most addicts, you are what I call "terminally unique." I know that I was. I could look at another addict and explain to you all the ways in which I was different from them. Most addicts think the general wisdom of recovery doesn't apply to them because their experience and situation is so specific.

Because of this, at some point, the rigidity of a program will feel restrictive. You will complain about the way it works, about the things you are being asked to do. You will question, "Considering my *unique* situation, is all of this really necessary?" It's a way of deflecting or avoiding. It's a lie you will tell yourself to sabotage your progress or protect yourself from the hard parts.

Again, the promise made in Step 2 will be important in these moments. As it gets tougher and tougher, we can remind you, "This is your commitment. You came to us. You made this commitment to yourself. It's between you and God." You need to have done the work so that when the defensiveness kicks in, when you question our methods and motives, we can say, "If you can't be honest and forthright with yourself, how are you going to be honest and forth-right with us? If you can't even keep the first promise you've made to yourself, to be willing to change, then how can you keep any of the other promises to come?"

If you are not an addict and are not sure how to relate to this struggle, think about what it's like to begin a diet, especially for health reasons. Maybe you've had a scare or just had enough of your pants not buttoning up. You acknowledge that genetics might make things more difficult, but this is your problem, and yours to fix. You look at yourself in the mirror and determinedly say, "I'm going to make a change." You may even be excited to get started.

But how does it feel when the reality sets in? "Oh, wait. I have to eat less? I have to go to the gym more? I have to spend less time in front of the computer and television?" The actions you have to take on a daily basis are less exciting than the declaration of intention. You need to be able to return to that inspiration, to that plan you made for your health and your future.

It's not easy, but without the commitment from the outset, it's next to impossible. And that is just a fraction of what a person struggling with their addiction goes through, and why the Second Step is so important to staying on the path.

Change Is More Than Skin Deep

At Haven House, we have a wide variety of men from very diverse backgrounds. Some come from wealthy, high-status families, and some have been living on the street, possessing nothing and connected to no one. As I've said before, addiction does not discriminate based on economic status, so neither do we.

As a result, a lot of guys come into Haven House looking rough—months and years of drug use will do that to a person. Their clothes are a mess; they're unkempt, unshaven, and sometimes unbathed. One of the first things we do is get them cleaned up. We ask them to shave and shower and give them a haircut. If they don't have anything decent to wear, we pull some clothes from our stores and get them dressed. And I don't mean run-down, threadbare, secondhand clothes. We get like-new donations of Polo, Eddie Bauer, Cole Haan, and other top menswear.

However, we don't only clean you up when you've come off the streets. Our program requires a certain standard of appearance for everyone. All of our residents are clean-shaven, with short hair and a tucked-in shirt. These and other rules last for their entire stay with us and hopefully a lifetime. Self-respect and a presentability is very important.

It's great to see some of our residents who have never used an iron (we've taught many to iron) taking pride in their appearance for the first time. It is important for self-esteem and socialization. But a lot of them think *that's* change. They look at themselves in the mirror and think they are different people because they got a haircut and changed their shirt. It takes a while before they understand that what you look like on the outside actually has little to do with the change that is coming. When we talk about the kind of change Step 2 requires, we are talking about the emotional, spiritual, and mental change that comes from months of work, soul searching, and study.

When we talk about the kind of change Step 2 requires, we are talking about the emotional, spiritual, and mental change that comes from months of work, soul searching, and study.

If only it were as easy as pressing your shirt and straightening your tie.

So why do we require the outward presentation? We are preparing our guys for what it means to be disciplined. Some men really appreciate the shave and a haircut; some are defiant and angry about it. I have had men walk away from the program when I have told them they need to cut their hair or take out their piercings. I am not telling them that they need to stick with this look for the rest of their life—hair grows back, and piercings reopen. Certainly, clothes can be changed. But still, some people find it a bridge too far to follow these rules, and that tells you a lot about how committed they are to getting their life back on track.

Our dress code and requirements are primers for our program. They are a way of saying, "Follow these rules for a while. Do some things you might not want to do or have never had to do before. Because if trimming your hair or tucking in your shirt is just too much of a challenge for you, how will you follow through on your commitment to change when things get *really* tough?"

Changing the clothes and appearance is just one of the ways we prepare our guys for Step 2. When they come to us, we give them some time to settle in. They get accustomed to life in the program; they figure out their chores and jobs and tasks. And the whole time, they're doing the work, reading the *Big Book*, reading the Bible, meeting with sponsors, praying. Throughout this time, we're talking a lot about what it means to change. What will it look like? What kinds of things will have to change? Are they ready for it? They are giving their personal testimonies at meetings and hearing from others, many who are at different stages of recovery. All of this is mental preparation to take the next step and commit to changing their life.

How Is This Different from the 12 Steps?

In the traditional 12-Step program, Steps 2, 3, and 4 are as follows:

- Step 2: We came to believe that a power greater than ourselves could restore us to sanity.

- Step 3. We made a decision to turn our will and our lives over to the care of God as we understood him.

- Step 4. We made a searching and fearless moral inventory of ourselves.

In case it's not obvious, God and spirituality are *very* important parts of our program. The notion of a "higher power" is vital to recovery, and despite the fact that this new version of the steps function a bit differently, we are certainly not skipping Steps 2 and 3. We talk about God all the time in the program; no one will be surprised by his presence. I wear a cross, and we have prayer time and Bible studies and attend church on a regular basis. We are not hoodwinking anyone into thinking spirituality doesn't play a role. However, our new formation of the steps integrates the role of religiosity and devotion throughout the process, so that a person can discover and immerse themselves at their own pace.

Why? Well, for one thing, we have a lot of people who come to us who don't believe in God when they walk in the door, and we don't want to place a stumbling block before them, by making it impossible to get past Step 2. It doesn't matter what you believe; if you want to come and get help, you should be able to come and get help. You don't believe in God? That's fine. We're still going to talk about him; he will still be a part of the process. But you can wait—see if, how, and when your heart opens up to the possibility.

The traditional Second Step puts undue pressure on a person, saying, "God's the only way you can get out. You've got to realize that now, and you can't move forward until you do." That's limiting people, and we don't want to do that. We're ultimately saying the same thing in a different way—a way that won't put people off that we want to help.

We also get people in who say, "I already believe in God, but so far, my belief in him has not fixed me. I still ended up where I am. How is this going to help me now?" For that person, it's important to remember that his belief in God *will* play a role, but the whole process is not dependent just on God; he already knows you need to change. He's just waiting for you now. It's dependent on the individual's willingness to ask for help to change. This is an inside job between you and God. When we get to Step 3, "I'm ready to learn who I really am," we're going to talk more about who the addict really is and what his relationship to God looks like. But getting into the program and taking the step is not contingent on whether he believes, or on the nature of his particular belief system.

> **The whole process is not dependent just on God; he already knows you need to change. He's just waiting for you now.**

For the first thirty to sixty days they are with us, our residents are in classes every morning and every evening. During the day, they work. They go to Bible study, prayer sessions, group meetings, reading groups, and so on, and they have one-on-one time with their sponsors. They're immersed in their "moral inventory," and all the while, their minds are becoming clearer and sharper as the fog of drug use clears.

And only after a month or two of this information gathering, self-reflection, and mental and spiritual preparation, are they able to take the next step. Step 2, "I am ready to for change in my life," is the active, goal-driven outcome of taking the moral inventory detailed in Step 4 of the traditional 12 Steps. It's all there; it's just reconstituted into something more proactive and inclusive.

Learning to Stand on Your Own Two Feet

As you may have gleaned, our program is very rigidly structured. We have rules about how you present yourself, how you speak to residents and staff, how you spend your time, how you make your bed—the list goes on. From about six o'clock in the morning until your head hits the pillow, you are busy, engaged, and working toward self-betterment.

This formal structure is important for a lot of reasons. For many of the men coming to us, they need the constant stimulation. You know the expression "Idle hands are the devil's workshop"? The same goes for brains. If we can keep our guys active and distracted, especially in those early days, we are combating the powerful emotional and mental pulls addiction has on a person.

The structure also presents a stark alternative to how they have been living prior to this moment. The chaos brought on by a life of deceit, intoxication, and often criminal behavior can be exhausting and unpredictable. Introducing a stable, consistent environment, one that is focused on learning, good works, and self-reflection, is often a relief for our residents.

When a man arrives at Haven House, he is put into our structure in a supported and systematized way that ensures compliance—at first. His "big brother" will make sure he wakes up and arrives everywhere on time in the first week. He watches as the other residents share their stories and throw themselves into their tasks and jobs. He is told what to read and study and what to think about through his classes and meetings. In the beginning, he doesn't have to make any choices for himself; the structure is a no-brainer. For most of our guys, this is what they need: unwavering direction, as though they were children.

Eventually, gradually, this will turn into self-motivation. Seeing a different mode of living, understanding how life *could* be, and witnessing other men doing the work will make a person think differently about what their future can look like. All of this is leading up to Step 2 and making that commitment to change.

Because, like the shave and the haircut, just living within the structure of the Haven House is not making real change. It might *feel*

Seeing a different mode of living, understanding how life could be, and witnessing other men doing the work will make a person think differently about what their future can look like.

like change because it is so different. Waking up to an alarm and showing up to your job on time, being present at all your meetings—they are all significant steps in the right direction. But as long as you're doing it because we've told you to do it, it's not real change until it all clicks into place and a person can say, "Here's the big picture. Here's why I *want* to be up before 6:00 a.m. Here's why it's *important* I throw myself into my work. Here's why I *need* to do this for myself."

When a person owns their reasons and is motivated to make his own changes, that's when the real work begins.

We've updated this step a bit to make it more proactive. Committing to change might seem like a mental exercise rather than an activity, but it is actually a huge step that takes weeks of preparation and no small amount of courage.

Here are some things to keep in mind as you consider Step 2:

- For an addict, change is the scariest thing. They would rather face all kinds of terrors than commit to changing their lives or face who they have become.

- Some people think the "change" is learning how to change everyone around them. Other people might be contributing to the situation, but at the core of your addiction problem is always you, and that is what needs to change.

- Being at the center of the problem means being at the center of the solution—it's time to clean up your side of the street.

- Step 2 is committing to change—it doesn't mean you'll have to change your whole life in a day.

- Making a commitment is essential to staying the course. Your resolve will be challenged, and you will need to return to this promise throughout your recovery.

- Pressure can work for and against you. It can serve as motivation, but it can also serve as a stressor.

- Step 2 is important in identifying the reasons for making change in your life—it is essential for the big picture.

- Addicts are "terminally unique"—they think their situations different from everyone else's, so the general wisdom will not apply in their case.

- A dress code is about more than presenting an outward appearance of self-respect—it is a primer for following the rules and developing discipline.

- Unlike the original 12 Steps, our steps do not force acceptance of a higher power early on—spirituality is immersed throughout.

- We don't want to prevent people who need help from seeking us out. We let people discover their spirituality at their own pace.

- Many addicts already believe in God. For them, it's important to emphasize that the whole process is not dependent on God but on their own willingness to change.

- It takes a while to build up to Step 2—a person has to experience discipline and understand what a changed life looks like before they can commit to make that change.

STEP 3:

I Am Ready to Learn Who I Really Am

In order to truly move forward with your life, you have to take a hard look at the person you have been throughout your addiction and compare it to the person you really are. Who is the person behind all of the self-idealization, the lies, the bad acts, and the defense mechanisms that have risen up to protect your addiction? This is the moment to find out.

This step might come as a surprise. "I *know* who I am," you might think. "I've never pretended to be someone else."

But if you are an addict, there is almost certainly a disconnect between the person you project to the world, the person you *think* you are, and the person who you truly are inside. Chances are, you have spent so much time lying to and manipulating the people around you that it's possible you have begun to believe your own lies, your own false projections, and your own negative self-image.

Step 3 is about shedding the lies we've been telling ourselves and everyone else. It's about wading through the things we have done—separating, organizing, and getting it all straightened out—so we can understand what we did, why we did it, and who we are underneath it all.

After all, who is a person that can steal from her own grandmother? Who is a person who can drain his child's college fund? Who is a person who can lie to everyone in his life and somehow justify it as a necessity? When an addict begins to examine who they really are, these are the questions they have to ask themselves.

The task here is twofold. It is important to own your behavior, face the truth of your actions, and understand why you acted the way you did. But it's also important not to get lost in the despair of past acts and how terrible they may have been. The key is to somehow be honest with yourself and everyone else about who you have been without giving up on who you will become.

It's a fine line. You don't want to fall too far into self-flagellation, but avoiding the reality of what you have done is not healthy either. I can't begin to tell you how often I have listened to a person recount a betrayal or criminal act he perpetrated, immediately followed by the statement, "I'm really a good person."

It's true that he may have the *potential* to be a good person, and he may have been a good person in the *past*, but being an addict has clearly knocked him off that path. Facing the truth is the first step in getting back onto the straight and narrow.

Relationship to Self

For every human being, our relationship to ourselves is very complicated. For a person struggling with addiction, it is even more difficult to differentiate between the person we pretend to be, the person we *think* we are, and the person at our core.

Drug addicts have huge egos. They have spent so much time thinking that they are right, and that if people would just listen to them and do things *their* way, everything would be fine. They believe they have everything figured out. But all of this ego does not mean that they love themselves. As I often say, "Does a person who really likes herself kill herself slowly on a daily basis with drugs and alcohol? Does a person who loves himself allow himself to become isolated, alone, living on the street?"

A lot of addicts wouldn't let a dog live the way they have gotten used to living. They wouldn't want their sister or neighbor or nephew to live that way, but they have come to accept it for themselves. Somehow, despite having all the answers and being the center of their own universes, they do not truly love themselves. Facing this truth can be difficult.

Crafting an Idealized Self

Addicts have been hiding from who they really are for years, sometimes decades. In order to do that, they have had to form a skewed self-image, something we call an "idealized self."

> **Addicts have been hiding from who they really are for years, sometimes decades.**

Every person in the world has an idealized self. It's the way we see ourselves in our mind's eye, what we imagine when we think about ourselves in third person. Whether we

39

consider ourselves to be a dedicated parent, a shrewd businessperson, a selfless community volunteer, or a serious academic, most of us have placed the bulk of our self-image into some main identifying trait. For most people, having an idealized self is harmless. It reflects who we strive to be, how we hope the world sees us, and for the most part, who we actually are.

But for a drug addict, the idealized self is wildly out of sync with reality. It is either out of date, off base, or just deeply unhealthy.

Here's an example: I was sitting in on the intake for a new resident, and he was bragging to me about what an incredible salesman he is—how he has won contests, made huge commissions, and was even promoted in record time. "In fact," he told me, "within three years of starting as a salesman, I was running the region."

I listened carefully to the way he was speaking about himself, and I said to him, "According to this timeline, you haven't worked as a salesman in six years."

"That's right."

"So what have you been doing for the last six years?"

"Well, I lost my job and became homeless when I started drinking."

He had been homeless and a drunk *twice as long* as he had been a salesman, but thanks to his idealized version of himself, he ignored those six years altogether. I'm not saying he will never again be a successful salesperson or that he shouldn't have hopes and dreams to work toward. But part of learning about who you really are has to include the time you have lost to addiction. That time says something about you, even if you would prefer it didn't.

We often see a disconnect with addicts who are also parents. They will tell you until they are blue in the face that the most important things in their lives are their children. Meanwhile, their children have been taken away, or are living with grandparents, or have been neglected.

While some idealized versions of ourselves are aspirational, others are actually very negative and self-destructive. A person can create a whole identity around his sexual conquests and how many women he can consort with. A person can also get completely caught up in material things, what kind of car she drives, how expensive her watch is, what designer clothes she has in her closet. When all that is gone—when they no longer have the booze-filled confidence to chase women, or when they've had to sell everything to keep their addiction going—they suddenly have nothing left in their life. Everything is meaningless, and all purpose in their lives is gone.

The truth is, when you're an addict, almost everything else about you becomes eclipsed by that fact. For the time you are addicted, it becomes the dominating aspect of who you are. It dictates how you behave, how you interact with your family and friends, what your moral compass will allow you to do, and how you feel about yourself. When you have been an addict for five, ten, or twenty years, *that is who you have been that whole time.*

So Who Are We, Really?

If you have ever known an addict, you have heard or said something similar to the following statements: "She's so talented if she could just stay clean," or "He is such a terrific dad when he's not using," or "She's a totally different person when she's off the drugs."

The thing about these statements is, they're likely true. Sometimes it is a parent or spouse trying to make the situation sound less dire than it really is, but for the most part, addicts do tend to be very smart, talented people. The problem is they have been wasting all of their talent and intelligence on keeping their addiction going.

The person being described by that hopeful family member, the person underneath it all who is kind, and smart, and full of potential—that's the person we want to help addicts find. This step is about helping them remove all the selfishness, self-centeredness, stubbornness, and everything else getting in the way, to show off that person they were made to be.

When examining who you really are, the most important lesson to learn or be reminded of is that we are all children of God. It doesn't matter what religion you belong to, where you're from, or what you believe. We are all here to fulfill God's purpose for us. We may never know exactly what that purpose is, but that's not what's important. What matters is that we are confident in his love and plan for us. As long as we live our lives as best we can and help each other, we'll fulfill that purpose without ever knowing fully what it is.

So many of the addicts I see have what we call "a God-sized hole" in their lives. More than *anyone*, they need to believe in God's love, to put God back in the center of their lives. But it is often the people who need it the most who find it the hardest. Many of them no longer believe they are worthy of God's love. Some feel abandoned by God. Others have just never figured out the way to worship or believe in him. But in the end, *accepting yourself as one of God's children is the most important self-realization you can make, especially on the road to recovery.*

Why? Because any other formation of your identity can eventually fail you.

> **Accepting yourself as one of God's children is the most important self-realization you can make, especially on the road to recovery.**

If your whole identity is about your job, where are you when you lose your job? If your whole identity is about your children, what happens when they grow up and don't have time for you? If your whole identity is around sexual conquest, what happens when you age and are no longer as active or appealing as you once were?

Any notion of identity that you can wrap yourself around can be taken away at any moment. You can lose your physical prowess, your wealth, your family—almost nothing is guaranteed forever.

There's only one thing that will always be true, no matter what: you will always be a child of God. Literally nothing can change that. It's the only constant you can always count on. For a group of people like addicts, for whom change and instability is very hard, having that constant at the core of their identity can be the difference between life and death.

Drug addicts are usually in some sort of arrested development and have never fully gotten out of their adolescence; that is why so much of what we do at Haven House is reparenting. Part of Step 3 is helping our residents touch base with who they were before the drugs and alcohol dominated their life. What were their interests? Where did they find hope? Where did their spirituality live? What dreams and goals did they set aside? We help them try to touch base with the person they are underneath all the years of hard living.

Sometimes uncovering who you really are can be a painful experience, and not only because you have to face all you've been missing, or even all that you have done. Sometimes it means facing traumatic memories that you have been trying to avoid for years.

Over my years working with addicts, I have encountered people who have been doing drugs with their parents since they were children. They became Dad's drinking buddy when they were nine years old, or began using drugs with Mom when they were twelve.

A person who is pulled into addiction at that young age does not have a foundation on which to build a self-esteem, a core personality. For them, Step 3 is starting from scratch. At Haven House and other programs like it, an addict has twelve months to connect to something larger than their own sad history.

One of the difficult things to understand is that you cannot base your identity completely on your past, and you cannot place it completely on your future. You have to also be able to sit with the person who you are today, in this moment, when the "former you" is gone and the "future you" has yet to form.

> **You cannot base your identity completely on your past, and you cannot place it completely on your future. You have to also be able to sit with the person who you are today.**

The Bible says in James 1:4, "Let perseverance finish its work so that you may be mature and complete, not lacking anything." Addicts have never been taught how to persevere. They have developed the habit of quitting at the first bump in the road. This step is about learning how to begin to build that inner strength through the introduction of order, structure, and discipline. For many, it's the first time in their lives anyone has demanded this from them, and they do become more self-confident. They begin to develop self-esteem by doing estimable things, and by remembering they are always children of God.

Every person has examples in their lives that we can point to and say, "There you are. That's you. That's the person you want to uncover." Up until now and throughout recovery, we are getting to know them, drawing out their stories and histories, and learning about the times when they were sweet and decent, when they were happy, when their family enjoyed their presence. We remind them of the positive things and encourage them to work hard to make sure the good outweighs the bad.

The Challenge of Learning Who You Are

Change can be scary for anyone, but for drug addicts, it is terrifying. The fear of the unknown is a powerful deterrent from sobriety, and when a person decides they are going to change and truly learn who they are, they are choosing a new path. They don't know what it will mean for their future, what their lives will look like, or who they will be at the end of that path. It can be very intimidating, and we lose a lot of residents at this stage.

One of my favorite stories in the Bible is about the Israelites, just on the verge of entering the Promised Land. They had been freed from slavery and had been wandering the desert for forty years. Just as they were finally about to return to their homeland—a moment they had dreamed about for generations—what do they do? They panic. They decide to revolt, kill Moses, and head back to Egypt to be slaves again: "Let's kill our leaders, turn around, and go back to what we know!"

After everything they'd been through, going back to slavery seemed like a better option than the unknown. They didn't know what it would be like, and that scared them almost to death.

With addicts and alcoholics, the same powerful fear is at work. Because they don't know who they are at their core, they don't know who they will be when they don't have the drugs or the addict lifestyle to lean on.

Sometimes a person will look for an easy fix. They will try to lay an identity over themselves in a superficial way in order to skip the hard work of really sorting out who they are. We see it at Haven House all the time. People enter our God-centered, Christian facility and think, "OK, I'm going to be a Christian now," and they think their work is done. "God's going to love me, and I won't have any more problems."

Occasionally, I have to remind them, "Look, I'm a Christian, but if I don't pay my electric bill, they're turning the lights off. And the Lord will still love me, but he'll love me in the dark."

Again, we are dealing with men with a juvenile mindset and trying to help them find that maturity. Part of that is accepting the nuance of every situation—there is no one-size-fits-all solution or identity that will transform your life. Uncovering who we are, finding the good within ourselves, accepting ourselves as a child of God, a Christian, and any other mode of identity takes time, and discipline, and patience.

The Bible teaches us that no one is perfect; no one is all good except for God. The rest of us are a collection of good and bad habits, good and bad traits, good and bad histories, and chances are, we're going to mess up. This is one of the hardest lessons of Step 3. The addict mindset—the overinflated ego and self-centered attitude—leads them to think they can fix it all at once. Now that they've come to understand they are a Christian, they think they can also control the rest of their existence. It's truly a conundrum. They think "becoming a Christian" will solve all their problems, but in fact, they are still at the center of their own existence, trying to control a situation.

Expecting perfection of oneself, as many of our residents do when they come to get clean, will only lead to disappointment, self-flagellation, and often, relapse. There is a delicate balance here of encouraging that spirituality, fostering that love of God, fanning the flame of the Christian life, but not hanging every hope and dream on that being the solution to every problem. It is also a balance between accepting our flaws and imperfections, and all but predicting failure in sobriety. *There has to be room for making mistakes in life without returning to drugs.* The same way we have to show them who they are without telling them they are the worst person ever, we have to give them room for human failure without making relapse part of the process.

There has to be room for making mistakes in life without returning to drugs.

Of course, Rome was not built in a day, and constructing an aqueduct is easy compared to building a new self-esteem and realistic, healthy self-image. At Haven House, we have twelve months to help our residents learn who they really are, and the process is rarely a straight line. It is a methodical, slow, deliberate process. This is the Third Step, but it occurs in degrees throughout the entire process of recovery. In fact, understanding who you are, coming to terms with it, and feeling good about it can be a lifelong process. Step 3 is just about solidifying the tools and perspective to make sure you are heading in a healthy direction.

When I started the Haven House, I drew a stipend of $200 a month, and I drove a $500 car. I had almost nothing but my sense of purpose and hope for the future. Now I have a home, a family, a retirement account, and a nicer car. I wouldn't say I was happier in the old days, but there are moments when I feel nostalgic for the simplicity. Sometimes it's easier when you have a clear goal, when you know what you're doing every minute of every day. It is definitely easier to know who you are in those times, and that is the simplicity that comes with being in recovery.

How Is This Different from the 12 Steps?

In the traditional 12-Step program, Steps 4 and 5 are as follows:

- Step 4: We made a searching and fearless moral inventory of ourselves.

- Step 5: We admitted to God, to ourselves, and to another human being the exact nature of our wrongs.

In a way, Step 3 lines up well with both of these ideas. Being ready to learn who you really are involves taking a fearless moral inventory, and it means owning up to the exact nature of our wrongs. The moral inventory in our Step 3 is a little less formalized because it is an overall umbrella to these steps. Our guys are doing a lot of writing and talking throughout, and a more formalized inventory will be coming in Step 5. But Step 3 is about approaching this difficult self-reflection in a softer, more lenient way. It is about making statements, trying on new ideas, and developing new ways of thinking through meetings, visits, and talking.

Our Relationship to the Facts of Life

In some ways, Step 3 begins even before the First Step and goes on for the rest of your life. The first thing we do when someone enters the program is go through their history. "Tell me about yourself. How did you end up here? What did you do? Ever been in trouble with the police? What's the family history of addiction?" We collect all this information on day one, and these stories and histories are revisited repeatedly throughout their time at Haven House. They talk about it in one-on-one sessions; they talk about it in meetings; they talk about it causally with the other residents; and they talk about it throughout all the steps they go through.

Here is what is really interesting to watch: the facts of who a person is do not change. If Johnny began drinking with his mother at age twelve, we find that out on his very first day, and it's true forever. What changes over the course of twelve months is Johnny's relationship to that fact. His level of understanding, his level of responsibility, his level of acceptance will all change throughout his process through the steps.

This is true for the rest of our lives. The facts of where we come from, what we do, and to some extent who our families are—those are mostly fixed and constant. What we can affect, what we can change, what we can continue to grow and mature around, is our relationship to those facts, and how we let them affect who we really are.

This step is about creating a foundation on which we can form our identity for the rest of our lives. Here are some things to keep in mind when approaching Step 3:

- You have to compare the person you have been throughout your addiction to the person you really are underneath it all. What have you been lying about, to yourself and others?

- Having an inflated sense of self and properly loving and respecting oneself are not the same thing.

- The idealized self of an addict is wildly out of sync and can be harmful. The truth is, when you are an addict, that is the defining attribute of who you are for the time you are using.

- We are all children of God, and we are here to fulfill his purpose for us. Any other formation of your identity can fail; being a child of God will always be true, no matter what.

- Perseverance is key. Failure is part of the process, but that doesn't mean you have to return to drugs. You can make mistakes and continue on.

- The facts of our history and who we are do not change. What changes is our relationship to those facts and how we deal with them.

STEP 4:

I Am Ready to Be Different

U p to this step of recovery, we've talked about what it means to be a part of the problem, what we've done, and who we are. We've also started to take on some small, superficial changes: being on time, writing in journals, tucking in shirts. Throughout all of this, it has been slowly dawning on the residents that things *have* to change; our lives *have* to be different, and it is up to us to make that change. Step 4 is committing to that change, now that we have a deep understanding of what it is really going to look like.

This is an important step, because up until now, an addict might agree to just about anything, if it'll get them out of trouble. They're going along to get along. *This is the moment where they need to decide if they are really going to change their life.* The talking we've done up until now has been important—we've learned a lot and prepared for change. But when it's just talk, an addict can end up embellishing, or changing the story a little bit. They might have been softening the edges and deflecting some of the blame.

When they get to Step 5, they are going to have to start putting things down on paper, and once people start to see the details in front of them, in stark black and white, they have to take on the real responsibility for their life, and that's a different story. Step 4 is their chance to stop, take stock, and confirm they are ready to make this change in their deepest heart of hearts.

Preparing for the Next Steps and Beyond

In many ways, Step 4 is all about preparing for Step 5 and beyond. Up until now, we've been gathering so much information. Over the past weeks and months, we've been going through the steps, attending classes and meetings and prayer, and we've been collecting information about ourselves. A bigger picture is starting to emerge—we're starting to see the arc of the story up until now. We've taken the first three steps to recount, "Here's what I've done. Here's what I've said. Here's where I'm headed."

Now we've arrived at Step 4, and this is the moment we're going to commit to these things that we've learned. That commitment is going to help you get through these next steps—the inventory you're going to do, the deep dive into the spirituality you will need, the plan for the way you are going to live for rest of your life.

With this step, things begin to get more concrete. Here we are encouraging our residents to find time to read, study, and pray at least twenty minutes every morning and evening. It can be a guided ritual, or independent, depending on the person. A clear schedule is important in establishing a consistent attitude. We're going to be focused on prayer, on being decent human beings, and we're going to work toward this goal of cleaning up our insides, letting God in, and straightening out our lives.

From the beginning, prayer has been encouraged as part of the routine. And while belief in one religion or conformity to one way of believing is not required, it is increasingly important to adopt prayer as an attitude of opportunity.

I want to encourage you to not think about prayer as something "official," something you do just once a week, on bended knee, in a structured setting like a church. Prayer is a general state of mind. You wake up in the morning, and you say, "Good morning, God." You spend your day acting like somebody who talks to the Lord, and at the end of the day you say, "Amen." That's the end of the prayer. In 1 Thessalonians 5:17, the Bible says to "pray unceasingly," because if that is how you live, then your whole life is sanctified. For us, this is the attitude of opportunity—this is recognizing a second chance from God.

If an addict reads, studies, and prays each day and each evening, she is focusing on this attitude, and that is how it becomes a way of life. It is essential to stay in touch with that goal of goodness and decency throughout the day because, as the Bible says in James 1:24, "You can be like a man that looks in the mirror; for once he has looked at himself and gone away, he has immediately forgotten what kind of person he was."

It is also a chance to implement the discoveries we have made in Step 3, about who we really are and how that relates to who we want to be. Even as we are trying to be the best versions of ourselves, mistakes will still happen. At Step 4, we begin to talk about our missteps and work to counteract them.

The Attitude of Opportunity

For many addicts, it is hard to see the process of recovery as an opportunity. At first, it feels like an ending. Although they know they need to make this change, the commitment to being different seems like a door closing on everything they have known. It can be hard to reframe something so significant for people, so I like to tell a story about one of my heroes, Mother Teresa.

Mother Teresa was waiting at an airport to catch a plane, and her new assistant came up and said, "I have terrible news; we've got a problem."

"Oh my, what is it?"

"The plane is going to be delayed three hours," her assistant told her.

Mother Teresa, who had certainly experienced greater trials and tribulations than this, told her new assistant, "I've been praying for time to read this new book I have, and three hours is about what I need. Now, I finally have it. As long as you work for me, we have no problems, only opportunities."

What does it mean to adopt the attitude of opportunity? We have been asking for a certain attitude since Step 1, asking our residents to do daily reading, studying, praying, and attending of meetings. We have been asking them to be generous, be on time, look presentable. Up until now they have been doing these things for a variety of reasons. They want to fit in with the other residents, they want to stay put and not get kicked out, they want to see what it feels like, they want to be able to *say* they are making a change.

In Step 4, we are asking them to stop doing these things by rote, or by necessity, and commit to doing these things consciously and intentionally. Some addicts are earnest and sincere from the beginning. They already have the right attitude, so this step is going to reinforce that, to confirm for them, "Hey, I'm where I'm supposed to be."

But for others, this conscious commitment to doing estimable things is harder than it sounds. We have people pass through here who seem excited and dedicated, who do all the right things, until the staff looks away. Then their whole face changes. Their attitude crumbles. They talk poorly about the other residents; they disrespect the staff behind their backs or disparage the program in general. They never do it to our faces—they understand what they need to do to stay enrolled. But their heart is not really in it, despite the fact that they are going through the motions. We see this at Haven House, as I am sure it is seen in every recovery program in the world. It's part of the process for a lot of addicts.

As it says in James 4:3, "When you ask, you do not receive, because you ask with wrong motives." If a person is just going through the motions, pretending to make a change, she is going to get nowhere, because it's self-driven and self-centered. She is still trying to get out of it what *she* wants; she is still trying to control the situation.

Other people who are not yet showing the right attitude are not necessarily being duplicitous; they are simply negative. They feel put upon—that something is being imposed on them. Nothing is ever right; nothing seems to work. They come in having decided, "This is for everybody but me." It's hard for them to believe that this is worth committing to, that this will be the change they need. They have failed too many times before, or they have simply lost faith in themselves and in God.

The key is to commit to being different with an open heart and hopeful attitude. Appealing to prayer, even if you are not sure *how* it will work, will move you toward that changed attitude of opportunity. You cannot lie your way into a new life. But if you commit to the schedule, commit to the actions, and fill your days with estimable behavior, you may be able to *act* yourself into a new way of life.

I have heard the expression "Fake it until you make it," but that does not quite apply here. Even if you don't feel it on every level, it can't be faked. I think "Try it until you buy it" is more appropriate in this situation. Go through the actions, do the right thing, keep your heart open to possibilities, and the faith and spirituality will follow.

I know a pastor who told me a story about a fellow who was considering becoming a member of his congregation. The guy came to the pastor and said, "Look, I don't believe in anything you're preaching, but I want my family to belong to a church. I think you're a decent man, and I think they need it. Would it be a problem for you that I don't believe?"

The pastor told the man, "As long as the other members don't find out, it's OK with me."

About six months later, the same man approached the pastor again. This time he said, "I want to be baptized."

The pastor was surprised. It's true; he had seen him coming and going to church with his family every Sunday, and he saw how they were involved in charitable activities, how they participated in study and prayer. But he had not known anything had changed for the man in terms of his faith.

"I'm thrilled," said the pastor, "but what happened?"

The man shrugged. "I've acted myself into a way of living. It works for me, and I don't want to lose it."

You don't have to be 100 percent sure on every level. You just have to know what works, where you want to be, and how do to the right thing.

Preparing for the Darkness That Lies Ahead

At this stage in recovery, an addict might be feeling really good. They have made some superficial changes; they have adapted to the way of life in their facility or group; they are beginning to see what life without addiction might look like. This is the halfway mark of our Seven Steps, and it is no small accomplishment to have made it this far.

However, the steps that have yet to come are very difficult. Taking moral inventory, righting wrongs, even facing what freedom means, can be very frightening. (Remember what happened to the Israelites when they faced freedom at the gates of the Promised Land? They almost chucked it all and went back to slavery.) If you value the steps you are taking, if you are being truly honest with yourself and others, then the rest of this journey will be effective, but it will also be painful.

If you value the steps you are taking, if you are being truly honest with yourself and others, then the rest of this journey will be effective, but it will also be painful.

The remaining steps can bring you to a very low place again, so Step 4, as simple as it appears on its face, is an essential preparation to have the right attitude and to fortify yourself to move forward.

You have been fitting in up until now, going through the motions, and it may feel very genuine and authentic. But now you have to find that attitude in your darker moments—when you're alone, when you're waking up, when you're going to sleep, when you're alone with your thoughts.

Everyone has dark moments to reflect on. Everyone has behaviors they regret, conversations they wish they never had, betrayals they perpetrated, and mistakes they made. As we've established, no human is all good, and it's normal for any person to look back with a certain degree of regret—we've all got cringeworthy moments in our past.

The difference is, many addicts have *never* looked back and cringed. They have never admitted to doing *anything* wrong. They've made excuses and denials for everything they've done since they were twelve years old. They have years to look back on, take responsibility for, own up to. They have to start to take stock of everything they've lied about, everyone they've hurt. That's a lot to ask of a person. That kind of work requires some fortification.

There's a reason this step comes in the middle, after we've already been working on behavior for a while. We've been going to meetings, participating in church—we've been helpful and getting into the spirit of things for a good period of time so that when the time comes, we are ready to start tackling the big stuff.

You can't be sober for two days and dive in to your moral inventory. You've got to put in weeks, a month or two, taking the time to connect to the people around you, form bonds, learn trust. You've got to start at a higher point than when you first came in, because there is a long drop ahead of you, and you can't start low to the ground, or there will be no place to go.

Addicts tend to withdraw when things get tough. They become ashamed and embarrassed, and they become hermits. But if they have spent weeks connecting to the community around them, they are less alone. If they have committed to going to meetings, they can't just hide away. If they have been going to church every week and have the pressure of being expected the next week, they can't just stay in bed. There is a practical aspect to all this scheduling and behavior, and it is to stay connected when things get really hard.

> **There is a practical aspect to all this scheduling and behavior, and it is to stay connected when things get really hard.**

This is part of what it means to *be* different. Up until now, you may have followed your instinct to hide—from yourself, from your family, from your community. Now that you have made this commitment, you're going to do the opposite of what your instinct tells you to do.

I recently greeted a new resident in my office. When he came in, he still had a beard. I've mentioned before that we have strict rules about facial hair at our facility. Just a reminder: I don't have anything against a beard—there's nothing morally questionable about facial hair—we set rules for all the reasons I have already mentioned in this chapter. It's about committing to being different, going against your own negative instincts, about going along with rules and being disciplined. But here was this guy, already enrolled in our program, and he had not yet shaved.

The first thing I asked him was, "Why are you in my office with a beard? Weren't you asked to shave?"

"Yeah," he said, "but I didn't have time."

Any grown man with a face knows it does not take that long to shave. This was about maintaining a defiant attitude, not the number of hours in the day. I looked at him and I knew we had got our work cut out for us. He is a good example of why Step 4 is so important.

If he wasn't willing to take fifteen minutes to shave on day one, he wasn't going to be ready on to face his past on day two. He had miles to go before his attitude was fortified, before he was trying to be good and decent, and before he was connected enough to our staff, our facility, and our other residents.

He left my office, he shaved, and he came back into the room with a whole new attitude, but only time will tell whether following the rules will really change him. Hopefully, by the time he arrives at Step 4, he is following the rules out of the desire to be different and is committed to making a change.

One Step Forward, Two Steps Back

Because of all the reasons I have already outlined, we sometimes see people acting strangely during Step 4. This gets worse in Step 5, but it starts here as we prepare. Some residents may get a little squirrelly; they begin to be late, to be forgetful, to be a little edgy. Things are starting to get real, because soon, it will not just be discussions about their drug use or a focus on Bible study. They realize we're going to be talking about their sexual conduct, their relationships with their children, their marriages, their interactions with their parents. Some of them realize they are going to have to start dealing with a history of abuse, criminal activity, humiliating acts.

At Haven House, our residents understand what comes next, because they are seeing the people it's worked for—our graduates come back often to speak and spend time at our facility. They've seen the steps work; they know everything will be different on the other side of this process, and the pressure of that can really affect people. We see some people begin to get really short with others, expressing frustration, wanting to quit, crying, getting depressed—all of this because of the anticipation of facing their past, facing some harsh realities they haven't thought about since they were kids.

Don't forget, addicts are people who are hiding from everyone, including themselves. As they approach the truth, their true selves are also emerging. A guy who has always seemed cool and above it all is coming to terms with being a nervous wreck inside. A woman whose ego is so inflated has never let anyone know how much she is suffering is beginning to recognize she's trapped. Coming to terms with what it means for your life to be different can be the final straw for some people.

Keep this in mind: for some people, this reaction to Step 4 reveals an understanding of how life changing this process will be. If an addict is not taking the upcoming steps seriously, she might not be so nervous and thoughtful about what is coming. If someone is frightened, she is respecting the fact that the change that is coming is serious.

How Is This Different from the 12 Steps?

This step is somewhat unique to our recovery umbrella. It comes around the time we are addressing Steps 4 and 5 and takes a different angle, allowing for a moment of preparation. In the controlled environment of Haven House, we are able to take special care for these steps in anticipation of the big changes, making sure the attitude is in the right place, fortifying the commitment to the process, and hopefully, preparing our residents for more success. But in any process of recovery, a person can check in with themselves and be sure to mentally prepare for the difficult, but important, steps ahead.

Step 4 is unique to our specific process. On its face, it might just seem like a pause in the action, but we have found it to be a crucial moment in recovery. We're getting ready to commit. We're preparing to take moral inventory, and that means fortifying our commitment.

Here are some things to keep in mind for Step 4:

- Up until now, addicts will agree to anything to stay out of trouble. This is the step where they have to make a conscious commitment to change.

- A firm schedule of reading, study and prayer help us prepare for the hard steps that are coming.

- Prayer is an attitude of opportunity, and a general state of mind. It is ongoing and constant—a way of life.

- It is time to stop doing good, decent, and estimable things by rote or by necessity. Now you must commit to doing these things consciously and intentionally.

- You cannot lie your way into a new life, but you might be able to act your way in: "Try it until you buy it."

- You can't start moral inventory and righting wrongs two days into recovery. You have to form bonds of trust, do some estimable things, and gain some confidence before you can address your past wrongs.

- When things get hard, commit to staying connected.

- People can act strangely when they get scared, and step 4 can be very scary. This is a sign of recognition—recovery is getting serious, and there are tough times around the corner.

STEP 5:

I Am Ready and Willing to Right All Wrongs

ow we have reached Step 5, and in some ways, this is where the real work begins. In the *Big Book*, it is described as a real turning point. The book even says, "You may exclaim, 'What an order! I can't go through with it.'"

Let me start by saying: "Yes, you can. But it won't be easy."

Owning your wrongs is extremely hard for nearly *everyone*. People don't like to admit to character flaws, mistakes, or failings. For an addict, it is especially difficult. Addicts have spent years, maybe decades, deflecting blame off themselves for anything and everything.

"It's my wife's fault the relationship went south. If she would have just given me one more chance, everything would have been fine."

"I didn't really do anything to get fired; my boss has always just had it in for me."

"It was the stupid policeman who pulled me over for that DUI. I was just barely buzzed. Why aren't they chasing real criminals?"

For an addict, everything has been done "to" them; nothing has been done "by" them. Step 5 is about identifying the things they have done, taking ownership and responsibility for their actions, and making amends with those they have wronged.

Taking Inventory

This step involves taking some actual inventory, which means writing things down and keeping track. Throughout earlier steps we have been talking about our histories, actions, faults, and failures. Now we are going to go through these past wrongs meticulously and own up to our mistakes.

At Haven House, we use different worksheets that are common in 12-Step programs. A simple internet search will yield various versions of this kind of worksheet, but they all address the same general questions: What did I do? Who was harmed by my action? What part of me caused the action? What is the nature of what I did wrong?

When it comes to what you did and whom you harmed, only you can answer that question. The more honest and forthcoming you are with that information, and the more thorough the work, the more genuine the result. You will have to write down, in your estimation, exactly what you did and all the people it affected.

When it comes to the question of "What part of me caused the action?" most answers fall within the following categories:

- Self-will/self-esteem/ego

- Emotional security

- Pocketbook/material security

- Pride/defiance/independence

- Self-pity

- Self-reliance

- Personal relationships

- Social ambitions

- Sexual ambitions

- Financial ambitions

Understanding what drives these actions is an important part of owning them. Then we must think about the "nature of what we have done wrong." Those answers usually fall into one of the following categories:

- Selfish

- Self-seeking

- Dishonest

- Inconsiderate

- Frightened/Fear

- Lack of self-discipline/self-control

- Playing God/trying to control others

- Self-centered/ego-centric

It is around this time when we also begin to take inventory of our fears. Fear can play a huge role in why we use drugs and alcohol,

> **Fear can play a huge role in why we use drugs and alcohol, and it certainly plays a big role in why it is so hard to recover.**

and it certainly plays a big role in why it is so hard to recover. Up until Step 5, we have been talking and praying about our fears. Now we are going to write them down and face them. We provide similar worksheets for this exercise, asking the main questions: What am I afraid of? Why do I have the fear? Which part of myself have I been relying on which has failed me? What part of the self does the fear affect?

When it comes to which part of the self we have been relying on, the answers usually fall within the following categories:

- Self-reliance
- Self-confidence
- Self-discipline
- Self-will

When it comes to the question of which part of self the fear has been affected, the answers usually fall into one of the following categories:

- Self-esteem
- Pride
- Emotional security
- Pocketbook
- Ambitions

- Personal relations

- Sexual relations

The life and history of every addict is different, and I couldn't possibly get into the details of all the different ways in which people fill out this information. There are millions of permutations and combinations of mistakes and fears people have to confront when taking moral inventory, and each is unique to the individual going through the process. I provide the information above simply to let you know how specific and in-depth the confrontation of your past wrongs will be in Step 5.

Taking Responsibility

Despite every addict having a unique journey, there are some universal reactions you can almost always count on. If you ask an addict, "Who is responsible for this mistake you made?" the answer will always be somebody else's fault.

"Gary, you wrote down that you crashed your car, and it harmed your parents, who had to pay for the damage. So who's at fault for that?"

"Well, if they hadn't insisted that I get the car home that night, I could've taken a taxi."

"Dana, you said that you talked back to your boss and ended up getting fired, and that hurt your husband and kids. Whose fault was that incident?"

"I'm much smarter than my boss, and she was threatened. She was always picking on me. She drove me to it."

We hear things like this endlessly. At the start of this step, it is less about what they have done and more often about what has happened *to them*.

This is, of course, to be expected. You are not going to sit down with a drug addict and have him say, "You know what? I did all this stuff wrong. If I hadn't taken these drugs, then I wouldn't have overdosed, and I wouldn't have ended up in the hospital, and then my wife wouldn't have left me." *It's a journey to ownership.*

Because of this, it's sort of a trick question to ask, "Who is responsible for this mistake?" The answer is always the same, but it takes them a while to discover it. It's not a trick question we ask to catch somebody out or to be cruel; it's a trick question asked to demonstrate the wrong thinking that's going on.

One Sunday, I was giving a sermon, and I admitted to one of my weaknesses. I said, "Every time this happens, I find it really difficult." In that moment, I could take the temperature of every addict in the room just by looking at his face. The people who were ready they were nodding along, imagining their own failings, thinking, "That's right. Me too." Those who were not ready were looking at me funny. I could tell they were thinking, "How could you admit that out loud?" They aren't there yet. They are still blaming someone else for their weakness, hiding from themselves and everyone else.

In order for the process of taking inventory to work, an addict must be honest and forthcoming, and must confess everything. You have to own the stealing, the lying, the manipulation, the crimes, the neglect. *The only way to be free is to admit to it all.* Once you have fully owned all your wrongs and taken responsibility for your life, then the process of making amends can begin .

Confession is harder that is sounds. I always say, "The problem with addicts is they have a good mind but a broken thinker." They can't think straight because their reasoning has become warped. They've deluded themselves into a crooked, juvenile, defensive way of thinking. This defensiveness is not only to protect their addiction but also to protect themselves. They have to live in some sort of altered reality, or else when they face all the terrible things they have done, they might fall into a deep, abiding despair.

It is now the job of a sponsor (or, as we call them at Haven House, a Big Brother) to help the addict unwind the false logic, to take the lies apart piece by piece. It can be slow and painstaking to go through each individual instance and make sure they have a clear picture of what really happened. Sometimes the sponsor goes through all of it and then finds the addict has fudged some part or left something out that he really doesn't want to face. A sponsor will look at the details and the specifics and say, "Wait a minute. *You* made this choice. *You* said this thing. *You* could have done something different right here. I have been there. I promise you, it's your fault."

This is a powerful process on more than one level. Not only is the addict being forced to reexamine his own narrative and see himself at the core of the problem, but he is simultaneously seeing someone further along, a sponsor, who has taken ownership of his life and who is continuing to do so. It's a clue of what is to come—a continual state of taking responsibility and truth telling.

Any attempt to lie or omit truth or details will only fool one person: the addict himself. Understand that when you leave something out, you're not getting away with anything; you are just letting secrets and lies back in to destroy your life, and you will have to do it all over again.

We understand that if you've been lying as a way of life for a long time, maybe even your whole life, it can be a very hard habit to break. Ultimately, it's up to you to be honest. That's why we call it the "inside job." Having done this for so many years, I can sometimes tell by looking at someone, "Something is still bothering him; there is something he is not letting out." A sponsor who has gotten to know you and has heard your stories might also have an inkling of what is really going on. But no one can make you speak. No one can tell you the exact nature of your wrongs. You must be ready to face these things and to do so with an open heart.

Here's a little story that I sometimes tell to illustrate this point: A Bible teacher suspects her class is not doing all their work. She says, "Next week we are going to study Mark, the sixty-eighth chapter. It's a lesson about liars, so come back having read it." The next week came around, and the class shows up. She says to them, "We are ready to start our lesson about liars. Please raise your hand if you read Mark 68, as I assigned." Three kids raise their hands. She says, "Well, there is no Mark 68, so thank you for starting the lesson for us."

The thing about a liar is that one way or another, she will give herself away, and the biggest loser in that situation is always the liar herself.

Facing Our Fears

I mentioned earlier that we also do this exercise to uncover fears. Fear is a motivator for so much irrational behavior, and lying in the face of Step 5 is no exception. Confession will inspire great fear. That is often what keeps people from doing it fully.

In Luke 18:9–14 we find the parable about the Pharisee and the tax collector, who have both gone to pray in the Temple. The Pharisee is silently praying, "God, thank you for making me better than other people," while the tax collector can't even raise his eyes to heaven. "I'm such a sinner, God," he prays. "Please have mercy on me."

According to Jesus, only one of them is going home to God. Can you guess which one?

We have to face our confession with humility and honesty. The Pharisee is delusional, probably because he is protecting himself. The way he has been living is contrary to what he has been saying. He thinks his lies can protect him, even in the face of God.

That is where many addicts are at this stage. They are afraid to reveal themselves, even before God. They are terrified that if

We have to face our confession with humility and honesty.

they ever get to the true nature of their wrongs, then the world will see them for who they really are. *They* will find out the truth about *themselves*. They will have to leave the idealized version of themselves behind and own up to all failings, weaknesses, and lies.

Being "found out" is a powerful, if somewhat irrational, fear. It's pervasive in every aspect of an addict's life, and it leads to dishonesty in some of the strangest places. I see residents who are delusional about their abilities and skills all the time. If we need a shed built on the property, someone will step forward and say, "I can do it. I'm basically a professional handyman."

"But aren't you an accountant?"

"Yeah, but I am an expert at this. I am the best person to do it."

What can you say in the face of such denial? What we usually say is, "OK. Have at it."

Inevitably, it will come out, of course, that they can't do it. Sometimes they are so convinced of their own lie that this failure comes as a surprise to them. Their idealized version of themselves is so ingrained, it can take failing to hang a door or fix a hot water heater to get them to admit maybe they aren't God's gift to the planet.

Often people turn their fear into anger. "OK, maybe it's not my husband, or my parents, or my boss, or those policemen who are at fault. But it can't be me! Maybe God is the one to blame.

Why didn't he do anything? Why didn't he help me? Why did he make me this way?"

The fear of what is next is also a powerful and destructive one. At the bottom of all of these wrongs is the inevitability of change. If I admit that I have been living wrong, then I have to make a change in my life. For addicts, that is the scariest prospect of them all. Many would rather deny God's existence than do that. "If God doesn't exist, then I don't have to make a confession."

Like I said, this is not going to be easy, but only by owning our past and facing our fears can we hope to move forward. Only making a true confession can free us from the bondage of addiction.

Understanding What Has Been Done to Us

I want to take a moment to make the distinction between things that we've done, and things that were actually *done to us*. When I say "the addict is responsible for *everything*," I should clarify—there are exceptions to that. People have horrible traumas in their past that certainly contribute to their addictions and behaviors.

Some addicts have been physically, sexually, and emotionally abused. They had parents who forced them to use drugs, they had teachers or trusted family members who molested them, or they were the victims of other violent crimes. In my years of experience, I've worked with many men who've experienced this kind of abuse. I know that for most women, this abuse is often a shared reality.

Of course, no addict is responsible for these events, and part of this step is about working with them to separate out what they are responsible for and what they had no control over. Often, they can't take responsibility for the mistakes they *have* made, but they have spent their whole lives blaming themselves for the heinous acts perpetrated against them.

A huge part of recovery is recognizing that you cannot accept responsibility for things that have been done to you, but you must accept responsibility for the things you have done since then, and in response. Those are two very different things.

Making Amends

So we've taken our moral inventory, gone over it, and faced some pretty harsh truths. Now it is time to make amends. This is a new, difficult phase of the process that is often misunderstood. *Making amends is not just saying, "I'm sorry."* Most addicts have already said that a million times. But no matter how many times he's said, "I'm sorry; I'll never do it again," as soon as he's forgiven, he turns around and does it again—whatever "it" is.

> **A huge part of recovery is recognizing that you cannot accept responsibility for things that have been done to you, but you must accept responsibility for the things you have done since then, and in response. Those are two very different things.**

What we are going to do is approach the person we have wronged and say, "Mom, Dad, I understand I caused you a lot of pain. I cost you sleepless nights, and I cost you money. I was high and drunk, and those things were my fault, and I shouldn't have done them." We are going to lay it out, just as we have written it out.

For monetary debts, we will have worked out the numbers in advance. "I owe you this much for the money spent on drugs, the wrecked car, the legal fees, the child care, etc." But often there is no "paying back" what was taken from your loved ones. Sometimes you can only offer an admission that you recognize what you've done and a commitment to doing better.

The good news is, that is very often enough. Often, the people who you have wronged are looking for you to heal and be healthy—they will accept your apologies and plans for a new life and will start fresh along with you. But sometimes, they have been too hurt by your actions, and there has been irreparable damage that just can't be looked past. Either is possible, and you have control over neither.

Sometimes making face-to-face amends isn't possible. The potential controversy is too great—there's a physical or emotional risk. Sometimes you can't get ahold of someone because they've moved or are an addict themselves. In those cases, the addict will write a letter. She'll put everything down on paper, put it in an envelope, and keep it in a drawer, prepared to send it or hand it over when they see that person or when the time is right.

Sometimes the person you have wronged is no longer living. We encourage people to put that apology in a letter too. It's important to get it all down, to have that conversation, even if it is just one-sided.

You are committing to changing your life, to behaving differently from now on. And the truth is, that's all you can do.

Because ultimately, you can only ever *truly* control one side—your side. At this point you have worked incredibly hard to face your lies, your true self, the wrongs you have committed. Now you are doing the difficult work of laying yourself bare to the people you have hurt. You are committing to changing your life, to behaving differently from now on. And the truth is, that's *all you can do*. Whether or not the other person accepts your apology is out of your hands.

Of course, this is easy to say and hard to live with. We want the people we've wronged to forgive us, to recognize our apology, to move forward with us. But sometimes they can't or won't, and we can't blame them for that either. We do not encourage addicts to look for acceptance—in fact, quite the opposite.

The truth is, considering the things you have done during the time you were an addict, you should just be thankful that *anyone* will speak to you. That God has seen in his wisdom to allow people to forgive you is a small miracle.

This is the reality, but it doesn't stop people from craving that forgiveness and acceptance. When we feel ashamed and guilty, all alone in a crowded room, acceptance might seem like the only remedy. Here's where arrested development comes in once again. When we are twelve, thirteen, fourteen years old, acceptance is the most important thing in our lives. Think about your experience with peers at that age, how desperate you were to fit in, to be one of the crowd, to feel like you belong.

Well, many of our folks are stuck at that age. If they end up not getting that acceptance right away, then they feel like it's all been for nothing. It can be really debilitating. We have to come at it from a more practical point of view, a more grown-up point of view: expect nothing. Be glad if somebody shows up to visit with you, to hear what you have to say. That in itself is a victory, whether they accept your amends or not.

How Does This Relate to the Original 12 Steps?

Step 5 continues to relate to Steps 4 and 5, while also being the umbrella under which Steps 8, 9, and 10 will fall. These original steps are as follows:

- Step 4: Make a searching and fearless moral inventory of ourselves.

- Step 5: Admit to God, to ourselves, and to another human being the exact nature of our wrongs.

- Step 8: Make a list of all persons we had harmed and be willing to make amends to them all.

- Step 9: Make direct amends to such people wherever possible, except when to do so would injure them or others.

- Step 10: Continue to take personal inventory, and when we were wrong, promptly admit it.

You will notice that Steps 6 and 7 are conspicuously missing in this list. They are:

- Step 6: We are entirely ready to have God remove all these defects of character.

- Step 7: Humbly ask him to remove our shortcomings.

As always, it is not that these steps are not addressed and included in our program. God is a part of every day through prayer and spirituality. In fact, in the coming steps, we are getting ready to address his role in recovery more directly.

However, as I have said before, getting somebody moving and going in the right direction is hard enough. When you insist on making God a prerequisite, you lose people who are not ready. If we start out forcing people to admit to the exact nature of their wrongs to God, it might give them pause, especially if they are not yet sure what their relationship to God is.

We all know God is present and is a big part of the steps. We are not avoiding him in any way. We are just approaching the steps a little differently.

Step 5 as a Way of Life

Throughout this book, we are talking in terms of "programs" and "steps" because it is a language we are all familiar with. But the truth is, this process is a bridge from your old way of life to a new way of life. The steps are not so much pillars we reach and move past, but layers we put down in order to walk a new path. *Taking moral inventory and making amends are not steps we do once; they are a constant way of life.*

For many people this comes as second nature. They look back over their day and reflect on what they might have done wrong. They think about fights with their spouse and don't hesitate to say, "Honey, I'm sorry. I shouldn't have said that yesterday." This is just normal behavior for people who don't have these issues.

For addicts, we might know that is a good idea rationally, but we don't know how to implement it. Step 5 helps us to just start living it. The Bible says in John 1:9, "If we freely admit each sin and confess, God will forgive us, and he will cleanse us continually." In other words, he will forgive us and continue to forgive us. But if we weren't constantly making amends, living our life in a constant state of taking inventory, God wouldn't need to continue to forgive us. It would be "one and done." That's not the reality of being a person.

When we begin Step 5, we are taking the inventory of things we've done wrong to others, but it is about owning the things we've done wrong to ourselves too. We're making amends with our friends and loved ones, but we also have to come to terms with and forgive ourselves. Here are some things to keep in mind:

- Addicts have spent years, maybe decades, deflecting blame off themselves for anything and everything. Owning their mistakes is especially hard for them.

- Meticulously writing down what we have done, whom we have harmed, why we have done it, and the nature of our wrongs is essential to this step.

- At first, an addict will almost always think someone else is at fault for their past wrongs. It takes some hard work to get him or her to see that they are ultimately responsible for all of their past behavior.

- The only way to take responsibility for yourself and your life is to own it all. You must confess honestly and thoroughly. Lying will only slow down the process and make it less successful.

- Interrogating our fears is also an important part of this step. Fear drives many of our actions and also prevents us from facing the truth.

- Only by making a full confession can we truly be free.

- Making amends is more than saying "I'm sorry." It's taking responsibility, paying back what you owe, and being different from now on.

- Usually people are rooting for you and will accept your apology. Sometimes, they won't. That's not your problem. You have to clean up your side of the street and proceed with no expectations.

- Taking inventory and making amends are not steps we do once; they are a constant way of life.

STEP 6:

I Am Ready for Spiritual Growth

Now we have come to Step 6—the step that puts God at the center of recovery. Up until now, spirituality has been threaded throughout this process, present in many of the steps, and a big part of the practice of discipline and self-awareness. But Step 6 is the moment when God becomes the *focus*. Going through the motions, like attending church, going to Bible study, and paying lip service to God just to do "the right thing," isn't enough anymore—he can no longer be a superficial part of your recovery. Now, you have to lean in to a full understanding of God, accept Jesus, and understand that you are turning your life over to him. You have to be *dependent* on God, or none of the hard work you have done in the previous steps is going to last in the long run.

In some ways, developing a "dependency" on God might seem contrary to other goals of recovery. When we think of maturity, we think of being *in*dependent, of making it in this world on your own. Isn't that what most parents are trying to prepare their children for? Recently, I found myself saying to my own children, "All I want is for you to be able to survive and live on your own before I die. I'll die happy if I can just get you kids to be independent."

As I have said in previous chapters, so much of what we do at Haven House is reparenting. Our residents have never learned the fundamentals of maturity—coping, perseverance, and empathy. We spend a lot of time "growing them up," so to speak, helping them join the adult world they have somehow missed out on. In other words, we are helping them to become independent.

However, even though independence is an important part of the rhetoric, we don't *really* want to raise adults who rely on themselves and themselves alone. We want to raise people who can take care of themselves in basic ways, but who can also be relied upon by others. We want them to go school, go to college, have families, and have careers, and that means being a part of a new community at each step of the way. It means finding ways to fit in and get along with people.

So what we really mean when we say we want our children to be independent is that we want them to be less dependent on *us*, more reliable, and more available to their chosen communities.

Now, for whatever reason, this lesson has been lost on the people we see coming to our program. Their parents and loved ones have not successfully taught them to be independent, and as addicts, their dependence has warped into something dark and destructive. Addicts rely on drugs, of course, but they also rely on their families through lying, cheating, and manipulation. Families of addicts will hear, "Mom, I need you to help get me out of jail," or "Sister, I need you to help me pay my rent," but they will not receive any support from the addict in return. True maturity is not standing completely alone or never asking for help; it's knowing how to take help and reciprocate in a productive, nonabusive way. Our residents have never learned to do

> **True maturity is not standing completely alone or never asking for help; it's knowing how to take help and reciprocate in a productive, non-abusive way.**

that with their own families, so the first thing they need to do is develop independence from the systems that have allowed them to remain addicts.

As the famous poet John Donne wrote, "No man is an island," and this is true, especially for people in recovery. Just as real maturity means knowing when to ask for help and how to be a part of a larger community, spiritual growth is about learning how rely on God and how to be his friend.

Finding a Friend in Jesus

How does one become God's friend? The first step is understanding that it must be a two-way street. It has to be more of conversation than a lecture. It's hard to have a friend whom you don't really know, don't really talk to, and don't really understand. In order to have a real relationship with God, we have to dig deeper and take a look at what the Bible is really trying to tell us—we just can't live on surface. It's one thing to read the Bible and familiarize yourself with its teachings, but digging into scripture, wanting to understand it and looking at its complexity—this is real spiritual growth.

A lot of people are waiting for others to do it for them. They expect their sponsor, counselor, or Big Brother to provide direction or instruction on how to have a relationship with God. Here is where some of the notion of "independence" kicks in. You may not be able to do it alone, but the desire and impetus to find your spirituality has to come from within you.

If you had a friend whom you never called, spoke to, or even thought about without someone else telling you to do so, then do you really even care about that person? If you don't know about their background, their beliefs, and how they might react in certain situations, it is really a true friendship? That's the intimate knowledge we need to have in order to have a friendship with God, and it has to come from a deep desire within you to know him.

Many of the addicts we work with are used to taking shortcuts. They want to rush the process, cut corners, and skip learning how to be a real friend. They think, "OK, I've been reading scripture every day, and I've been praying a little bit, so now I'm a Christian." Up until very recently, selfishness and self-centeredness allowed them to put themselves at the center of their own universe, and it can be a hard habit to break. But if they have done the work to examine themselves, to face who they really are, then that spiritual connection they form with God can be real.

Again, being a friend means sharing yourself, and in order to do that, you have to know yourself. If you have a friend and all you ever do is ask her what she thinks without ever contributing, that friendship is going to be short-lived.

I always tell our residents, "You can lie to me; I'm human and far from all-knowing. But you can't lie to God. You have to be straight with him. You have to be able to talk to him, tell him what really bothers you, the crazy ideas that you have, your truest fears. You have to be truthful and honest and a real friend." As the Bible says in Numbers 32:23, "Your sins will find you out." In other words, you're not going to keep them hidden.

Once you open your heart to a relationship to God in a real and honest way, you will find it easier and more reciprocal. It says in James 4:8, "Come near to God and he will come near to you." But how can you start doing that if reading the Bible and attending church isn't enough? Taking that step closer to God is about being who you really are.

When It Comes to Prayer, Start Simple

Prayer and meditation are extremely important skills when developing your spiritual life. Any good friendship involves frequent correspondence, and prayer allows us to communicate with God on a constant basis. We encourage our residents to pray all the time. You pray when you wake up, and you pray before you go to sleep, and throughout the day you can use prayer to check in with God as well. It may sound like a lot, but why limit yourself to only speaking to God when you're in church, or to organized, predetermined prayers? A relationship means having an ongoing conversation.

Just like any other friendship, you're not going to chat about the same subject every time you pick up the phone. And just like any other relationship, your expectations have to be realistic about the progress you can make and the expectations you can set.

Here's an example. I had a resident who was working hard on his spiritual growth. In many ways, he was succeeding—but he still struggled with the role of prayer.

"I'm praying, but I don't feel like I'm getting anywhere with it," he confided in me.

"Why not?" I asked him.

"I'm not seeing or feeling any results," he said.

So I asked him, "What are you praying for in the morning and at night?"

"Well, I pray for my kids. I pray for the planet. I pray for world peace. I pray to end animal cruelty. I pray to help those who are hungry … " And the list went on and on.

"Time out," I said. "Those are all good things to pray for, but if you pray for a hundred things, how will you ever know if God answered one of your prayers? Who can keep track?"

"Why don't you try this instead?" I told him. "Just pray a simple prayer of, 'Give me peace of mind, and I'll promise, I'll get up; I'll work hard for you every day.' Then go to bed, wake up, and do the same thing. Now, go out and act like a man who asked God for help and work hard for him. During the day, then, you can pray for whomever and whatever you want, but at night and in the morning, pray for only for peace of mind."

The reason I suggest this is because when you get peace of mind, then at least you'll know where that came from. You didn't ask any human being, and no human being could do that for you anyway—only God. You're going to know it when that prayer is answered, and just like reciprocity in a friendship, it means you're also going to have to hold up your end of the bargain and get up and work hard for him every day.

This is why we teach a simple prayer as the place to start. Now, I am quite sure that every individual develops their own prayers and prayer habits as time goes on. But to start with, to develop the practice, we teach them to be simple and straightforward. We say to them, "Be truthful. What's in your heart? Start with that."

People are scared to be honest about this, because for many people, the truth in their heart is, "I don't know if this will work. I don't even know if God can really help me. Even though I really want it to work, I don't know how to pray, because I don't know if I believe in this."

What's wrong with *that* prayer? Nothing. The Bible says you can pray for your unbelief, so even *this* is scripturally sound. "God, I'm here but I'm lost. I don't even know if you're real. Help me." For some people, that's the place to start. Most people can't start at the end, with long, flowery psalms as their prayers. They have to start off with the basics. "God, I'm lost. Help me."

Being Met with Resistance

Despite the absolutely essential nature of this step, it is often met with great resistance. Some people are mad at God. They think God dealt them a bad hand and that it's his fault things have turned out this way. "If God wanted me to be happy, he'd make me happy." It's the same cop-out we encounter in Steps 1 through 6: it's a way to abdicate responsibility. People don't want to answer for what they've done. They're afraid to face the truth.

> **If we really repent, and our motives are pure, all is forgiven. What matters is what you do from this moment onward.**

But as I always say to them, the good news is, the bad news doesn't matter. God doesn't care what you did last year, last week, or last night. If we really repent, and our motives are pure, all is forgiven. What matters is what you do from this moment onward. If we're earnest and ready to work hard, God will grant us what we need to face the next day, and the next, and so on.

Now we have to move forward and not repeat our worst mistakes. As Jesus said to a woman caught committing adultery in John 8:11, "'Does anyone condemn you?' And she says, 'No man.' And he says, 'Neither do I condemn you. Go and sin no more.'"

It's that simple. No one expects you to be perfect. "Go and sin no more." There's nothing to be afraid of.

As always, something being simple does not mean it will be easy. Some people can never get over their resistance to spiritual growth. They are just never able to tap into a true belief in something greater than themselves. This can turn out to be a real problem. The best-case scenario is they will stay sober for all their lives ... but be miserable. Because true sobriety is about more than being sober of mind and body. It's about finding a deeper freedom. It's about being happy, joyous, and free in your soul. The only way to do that is through a spiritual life.

I have long believed that alcoholics and drug addicts are very spiritual human beings deep down. It's the reason that they are so susceptible to destruction when they get lost. Other people can do terrible things and not be bothered. You'll often hear about people who lie, cheat, steal, take advantage of their family and friends, and it just doesn't bother them. They don't need to get drunk or high every day to avoid the darkness inside.

Addicts are people who can't behave this way without consequence. It crushes their souls. These are highly spiritual human beings who have lost their way. I believe this is why this step is so essential to the long-lasting sobriety and happiness of our folks—they really desire it; they just don't know how to get there. So we keep it simple and straightforward for them. Pray. Do good work. Stay connected. Go forth and sin no more.

This doesn't mean that if people don't get it immediately, they will never get it. The road is a different length for everyone. For some it might happen in a matter of weeks or months. For others, it will take years. As long as they're doing the other steps, as long as they remain open to the possibility and keep trying, they just have to hang on. It's not up to us when people have their spiritual awakening. It's not a requirement for everything to click into place on a certain schedule.

Our relationship with the divine is a lifelong journey. Even once you've found that inner peace and are talking to God on a regular basis, that doesn't mean the work is done or that you'll stay there forever. The idea that you will settle in one place and always have the same relationship with God is an unrealistic expectation. If you're growing and maturing, it's always going to be changing.

So what if you've reached this step, and you just can't see how to break open that little space, that room that God needs to grow inside of you? I would ask you this: Are you willing to start with the simple prayer? Are you willing to just say, "Here I am. I'm lost. Will you help me?" or "I can't do it on my own—help me." Are you willing to just say that?

Maybe you can start by just getting on your knees. There's an old trick I used to hear about: throw your wallet underneath the bed at night. Get on one knee, put your wallet under there, and say, "Help me." In the morning when you bend down to pick it up, say it again. It might seem foolish at first, but it can help you if you struggle with the willingness to get down on your knees. This can be a real challenge for people, especially men—they can't bend a knee. They think it's beneath them. They think it makes them weak. It's a matter of pride. So trick yourself at first. Keep it short. Keep it simple. Just say, "Help me." You don't even have to address it to God. He knows you're talking to him.

The real question is, What do you have to lose? A night in jail? Another divorce? A sad and lonely life? A terrible, avoidable death? What is so great about how you're living now that is worth protecting, just because you don't want to bend a knee?

Keep it short. Keep it simple. Just say, "Help me." You don't even have to address it to God. He knows you're talking to him.

No One Does It Alone

Not long ago I was working with a new resident, Mark, and he told me he wasn't sure he needed everything Haven House had to offer. "After all, once I quit for three years completely on my own."

I had to point out to him, "Yeah, but did you *really* quit?"

He asked me, "What do you mean?"

"Well, if you *really* quit, you wouldn't be here," I said. "You stopped for a while, but you never quit."

Solitude is a disease people mistake for a virtue. Maybe it goes back to that fallacy surrounding independence. People are ashamed to ask for help—from their family, from a recovery center, even from God. Many people feel like they should be able to kick this problem themselves rather than place the burden on other people. On the flip side, they also don't think their addiction is hurting anyone else. They are so self-centered that they are unable—or refuse—to see the damage it is inflicting on the people around them. Part of opening up to God is accepting that you cannot do it alone. First you have to accept the help from the people around you, and then you have to open your heart to God.

This is hard for many people because they have become skilled at denying what is staring them right in the face. A person must be willing to look at their problems and acknowledge that they need a new set of principles to rely on. And what they find out is that Christian principles, when followed, are very simple. There are really not many requirements. Essentially it boils down to, "Love God and be decent."

Love each other. Love God. That's basically it.

Still, it takes a lot of work to get there and a lot of work to stay there. Self-deception is powerful, and it can only be overcome through order, structure, and discipline. We introduce our residents to this new way of life in stages: first the discipline of the Haven House, our rules and structures; then the discipline of the 12 Steps (as contained within these Seven Steps); and finally, the discipline of the Bible. As they incorporate some good order, structure, and discipline into their lives, it quickly becomes evident that this works and that the old ways did not. So we're building as we're going, adding layer upon layer.

But you can't just lay down a layer and walk away. Each layer requires maintenance and attention at all times. So if I seem to be repeating or overlapping when I talk about these steps, it's because I am. You're never really finished with a step, in the same way that you're not really finished after just reading the Bible. You study. You dig in. You continue that conversation with God, in the morning, in the evening, throughout the day, and every day of your life.

How Is This Different from the 12 Steps?

As I have noted, all of the steps overlap and intertwine throughout the process of recovery. Our Step 6 goes on throughout the entire experience, and this is where it culminates. In relationship to the 12

Steps you may be familiar with, it most closely correlates to Step 2 and Step 11:

- Step 2: Came to believe that a power greater than ourselves could restore us to sanity.

- Step 11: Sought through prayer and meditation to improve our conscious contact with God, as we understood him, praying only for knowledge of his will for us and the power to carry that out.

From the beginning of your recovery, you are always trying to move away from selfishness and self-centeredness. The shift is about transferring that faith from ourselves and our faulty logic to relying on God. It doesn't mean we're helpless or powerless. We're going to handle what we can in life, and there are a lot of things we can handle. We can be a part of a community, be a good member of our family; we can work and support ourselves and our dependents. But still, there will always be things that baffle us, confuse us, that hurt us, and we're going to have to rely on God to work those things out. It's those moments that we have trained ourselves to turn to drugs. But if we can turn to God instead, it gives us a chance to persevere. We're not going to quit. We're not going to give up. We have got to rely on God to make it through the trial that's in front of us.

Romans 12:3–8 says that when we came to believe, we were given the "measure of faith," and now it's our job to mature that measure of faith. If we never do, we will really be lost in life from time to time. Wouldn't it be so wonderful to always have faith to count on, to know it will be there when life is tough, to give God the control by putting him right in the center of our lives where he belongs? If the spiritual connection is real, then you won't want to have God's job. You will be more than happy to let him to do his job, and you can focus on doing yours.

Here are some things to keep in mind for Step 6:

- In order to make the work you have done long lasting and solid, you have to develop a spiritual inner life. This means forming a true, reciprocal friendship with God and learning how to depend on that relationship.

- Independence is not about doing it alone; it's about being a reliable adult in your community.

- No one can do it for you. Taking that step closer to God is about being who you really are.

- Be consistent and realistic about your prayer habits.

- Start with a simple prayer for peace of mind, or simply ask for help. Be truthful and pray for what is in your heart.

- True sobriety is about being clean in your body and mind, and free in your soul through spirituality.

- There is no set schedule for a spiritual awakening. If a person is sticking to the steps and living with order and discipline, then it could take weeks, months, or years. As long as they stay open to the possibility, there is hope.

- No one does it alone. First you must accept help from people around you; then you have to turn it over to God.

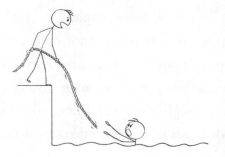

STEP 7:

I Am Ready for the Journey to Freedom, and I Am Ready to Help

O nce you reach Step 7, we're assuming that you've been through eleven of the traditional 12 Steps, have had your spiritual awakening, and are ready to get on with the rest of your life. Despite feeling accomplished and motivated, it's important to remember that you're not quite done yet.

Throughout this process you've been sharing your experiences, expressing your emotions, and practicing honesty. You have had a true change of attitude. A light has come on inside you, and it has made all the difference. You have been through physical, emotional, and spiritual change. You're overcoming all those selfish, self-centered thoughts, and you may have found that suddenly, you've put yourself third or fourth down the list of priorities. In comparison to God, family, friends, commitments, and responsibilities, you are a lot less important than you used to be. Yet it feels great, because you care about the well-being of everyone around you. Now, after all this work, we're ready to pass this good feeling and hope on to other people.

The importance of this step cannot be overstated. Of course, there are many people out there who need hope and guidance, and no one can relate to what they are going through as much as you can, having been through it yourself. But another equally important reason is that when you're helping others, you don't have time to focus on yourself.

This may look like a selfless act, and it is going to be a benefit to other people, but if you're truly helping others and interested in their well-being, it improves your well-being and your outlook as well.

We're All in This Together

Volunteer work and giving back is good for anyone's soul, but for a person who has been through recovery, it is really crucial to survival.

Volunteer work and giving back is good for anyone's soul, but for a person who has been through recovery, it is really crucial to survival.

They have to stay involved in community. Sometimes, when our residents are coming to the end of their time with us and getting ready to be out on their own again, I can tell that this reality has not necessarily broken through to their consciousness yet. They might be prepared to stick with the rules, discipline, and prayer they've gotten used to, but the real effort and attention that goes into remaining part of a community can be hard to maintain outside the program. We see it often; all of a sudden, the same person who may have doing great in the program starts to veer off. They start questioning the need. "Well, maybe I wasn't that bad. I can skip a meeting."

Or maybe they decide they want to try something different. A new meeting in a new place, just for the novelty of it. People are often drawn to the new, shiny object off in the distance. But as soon as they indulge in that craving, they've pulled away from the community that they matured in, where people know them and can point things out to them, and where they can be of help to others.

As people veer off the path and become estranged from community, inevitably they get into trouble again. This is why it is very important that you stay connected to people who know you, whom you've worked with, whom you've helped. Not only are these the people who know your history, who can call you on your lies and manipulation, but they also feel indebted to you for all *you've* contributed. When you have a history somewhere, everything can be a reminder of where you've been, where you are, and where you're headed.

Here at Haven House, we encourage our residents to stick around, remain part of our community, come back, and sponsor our residents. There is a range of involvement from our "graduates." Some of them join us for meetings, some come and have meals with us, some attend church on Sundays. Some just come back to visit, stopping in our thrift stores to say hi.

Of course, not everybody lives next door. We have residents who come from all over the country. When they finish the program, they often want to return home to their families. Still, we encourage them to call and visit regularly. We have one fellow who lives seventeen hours away, and he still finds a way to visit a couple of times a year and call us on a weekly basis. Modern technology helps too. We have people follow us on Facebook; they watch our church services on Sundays or tune into Bible study in real time.

As you'd imagine, having people who have been through recovery come back to visit and share their success stories—it's a big thing for our residents in treatment. Seeing people who have gotten on with their lives, who are holding down jobs, some even running their own businesses, and still staying connected to the community, gives them enormous hope about their futures.

What Does It Mean to Stay Connected?

As I said, we try to keep our graduates in the fold, to provide them with a community. But they can't always stay near us, and it's important for them to be able to create this dynamic wherever they are. Work, family, and life in general can sometimes force us to uproot and relocate, and we need to build the skills and experience to develop community wherever the wind takes us.

This is why we encourage people to go to church, Bible study, AA, or some other 12-Step meetings wherever they are. New in town? Don't know anybody? Find the local AA meeting and volunteer to set up the chairs, make the coffee, or stay afterward and help clean up. Maybe you live in a rural area, and you don't have any meetings close by. Think about starting one. Go even further. Think about finding out where the old folks' home is, and offer to drive residents to church, give them a ride to the mall, or help them run some errands. Show up at the animal shelter. Volunteer at a soup kitchen. Help out at an after-school program. Find a place that could use the help. Then get there early, and leave late. Keep these habits up, and let them remind you of what you're trying to do. It's the best a way to stay connected, whether you're close to us or not.

I recently spoke to a fellow named Stan who went through our program years ago. He has been doing well ever since, working in the field, helping others with recovery. Recently he went on a ski vacation with his family in Colorado. Stan was waiting in line for the chair lift with his son when another man struck up a conversation. When Stan told this other skier what he did, the other gentleman immediately launched into his own tale of woe. He had a sister who was really struggling with addiction. He was at the end of his rope and didn't know what else to do to help her. Stan knew he was the right person for this man to talk to. He rode up the mountain with him and then joined him in the lodge later for some hot tea.

"I'll be honest, this was not what I was hoping for when I woke up that morning to hit the slopes with my son," Stan told me very candidly. "But this fellow was clearly in distress and wanted to talk about his sister, so there I am, talking about his sister. Because it doesn't matter what I want; that's the next thing I have to do. And I don't resent it at all."

Part of maturity is also coming to terms with what Stan describes experiencing on the mountain that day: we all do things that we don't want to do because they know they are good for us. It doesn't mean we resent them, and it doesn't mean we're not going to do them. We go to the gym, we eat healthily, we go to the dentist. We do those things and don't get angry every time, because they are part of an adult life and we are able to see the forest through the trees.

That doesn't mean it's always instinctual. Who hasn't woken up one morning and thought, "I don't want to get up, so I'm quitting my job," or "I'm going to buy this car even though I can't afford it"? If you think you're alone, ask your mom if she ever had the thought,

"To hell with it all—I'm leaving my husband and kids and going to the beach." But after all that, what do most of us do? We drink our coffee and go to work.

It's not that you won't have moments where you think about it. Your brain is still your brain, and it will have instances where it wants to rebel. But maturity means doing the hard thing, the thing you might not want to do in that moment, because you can anticipate the consequences and want a certain kind of life.

Like sticking with a marriage, sticking with recovery comes from a belief in something larger than the moment you are in and larger than yourself. It's not about what you want in any given moment; it's about having a faith in an institution or a commitment to spirituality. It's saying, "I understand this is all part of a bigger picture. And even if I don't see the whole picture every moment, I'm always part of it."

There are many times in life it would be easier to put yourself first, act in your own self-interest, cut corners when it comes to being a part of your community. Being a consistent participant requires a lot of energy and discipline, and even people who start with enthusiasm can find it hard to maintain that momentum. It can become a slog.

The Bible says in Corinthians 3:2, "I gave you milk, not solid food, for you were not yet ready for it." There is an adjustment period that goes on for a long time. It's a new life, and on good days it's easy, and on not-so-good days it's difficult. For some people, they're doing it out of duty and to maintain a regimen, to get a return on investment, so to speak. That is usually only good for a short period of time, but we encourage them to keep going, because maybe they'll get it eventually.

The people who maintain those connections to a community, whether they want to or not, are the people who are most successful. I've seen people who are not involved with their community, who are not giving back, and sometimes they are able to stay clean, but believe me when I say they are miserable. They may think it's easier to resist this step, but what they are doing in reality is creating obstacles for themselves. If they make it, they are almost always hanging on by the skin of their teeth. And most don't make it. They withdraw, they become selfish again, and they implode. Sometimes, our connection with other people is the only thing that can prevent us returning to the old dynamic, the way things were, the bad old days.

It Takes One to Know One

When you help someone dealing with the same issue as you, you revisit your own weaknesses and problems. The old saying "If you spot it, you got it," is true; no one is better at sniffing out nonsense as someone who has dished it out before. Nothing is as powerful a deterrent as watching someone else suffer the way you once did. It reminds you where you never want to go again. I for one, recognize pretty much all the trouble areas, because I've had them all.

That's one of the many things I appreciate about the Bible. When I read it, I identify with the people in it because they seem real and flawed. They have weaknesses; they face hard times. And it speaks to me because I have been there. It wasn't until later in life that I got onto the right foot and could see how those experiences empowered me to help other people. I've seen some of our own residents make this realization when they become Big Brothers in the program. Of course, often these newly awoken addicts marvel at what it looks like from the other side. You'll hear them say, "God, that new guy is crazy.

He's out of his mind." And I'll smile and say, "Hey, I knew a fellow who was *just* like that once upon a time."

Our residents are sometimes with us for months before they embark on the actual steps, but they begin *living* the steps through practice and habit immediately. We are working on getting them used to that good order and discipline that will help organize their life and working up to the moment when they can truly say, "I'm ready." And just like the other steps, practicing being a help to others is part of this process. Within weeks of arriving, they are helping new residents as Big Brothers.

Our Big Brother program is probably the best preparation for Step 7, because it takes the addict out of the center of their own attention. Helping a new person find the laundry room, wake up on time, and adjust to life at Haven House is a distraction from the self. It requires them to be patient and kind with somebody, to practice selflessness, to return the favor someone has recently provided to them.

It also reminds them where they were, in some cases just a few short weeks ago. It illustrates to them how far they have already come and how instantaneously they can be back where they started. It is a constant reminder for them to say, "I am powerless," but also "I *do* have something to give back." Many of our residents arrive here thinking that they have no value to anyone else in the world. Being a Big Brother within weeks of arriving helps to build their self-worth.

Continuing that practice, we host a 12-Step meeting in our facility, and it is run by our residents. We open it to the larger community; people who aren't part of Haven House's program participate. Our residents learn how to lead, prepare, set up, and everything else involved in leading these meetings, and soon we are sending them out into neighboring areas to help run satellite meetings as well. They run them according to the tradition of AA, so anyone with a need, anyone who is traveling through the area or looking for a meeting to join will feel comfortable and at home. It also enables them to start a new meeting if they ever find themselves in a community with a need.

How Is This Like the Original 12 Steps?

This step lines up almost exactly with the original number 12.

- Step 12: Having had a spiritual awakening as the result of these steps, we tried to carry this message to alcoholics and to practice these principles in all our affairs.

Once we have learned to put God at the center of our lives, giving back and being a part of a community is the logical next step. Understanding that staying connected is our best chance to staying sober and whole will inspire a lifelong commitment to giving back.

Here are some things to think about as we approach this last step:

- No one knows what an addict is going through more than someone who has been through something similar.

- When you are helping other people, you have less time to focus on yourself.

- Connect with a community wherever you are. Go to church, Bible study, or the nearest 12-Step meeting. Get there early and stay late.

- Accept that you have to do things you might not always want to do. That is a sign of maturity.

- The people who stay connected to a community on a regular basis are the ones who will be most successful.

CONCLUSION

Are You Ready for a New Life?

Now that we have reached the end of our time together, it's a moment for some truth. Here's what I really think: if you've got it, you got it; if you don't, you don't. That might be hard to hear, because how do you know if you've got it? Well, the good news is, it's still up to you, and it's never too late to try. If you have failed in the past, it doesn't mean you'll never get it. It means you haven't gotten it yet. And today could be your day.

The 12 Steps of Alcoholics Anonymous say you can quit, and quit for good. That's what we believe, and that's how we approach every addict we encounter. It's within your ability to kick this habit forever—but only if you live through and learn the lessons of every single step. If you don't "get it," if you don't internalize the steps, take yourself out of the center of your universe, and turn yourself over to God, it's always going to feel like you're hanging on by your fingernails. In that case, you can do all the right things, maybe even hang on for a long time, but eventually you will fall. It's really that simple.

It's not an attack on anybody; it's not an accusation that anyone is not as good or not as strong. It's just the way it is.

Take the fellow I mentioned in our discussion of Step 6, Mark, who thought because he'd once quit for three years on his own he didn't need to be at Haven House, despite the fact that he'd relapsed.

He hadn't gotten it yet. But I haven't given up hope for him.

What makes people go back? Why do they relapse? The people we see are often desperate for change and believe they are doing their best to make it happen. Why would they throw it all away, especially after all the work they do to make it through the program?

We end up going back if we missed something the first time—if we weren't completely honest, or totally ready to turn ourselves over to God. If we are really honest with ourselves, if we really have a spiritual awakening, then there's nothing to cover up, and there's no way to go back. And even though we might worry about it, even if we have those very human moments where we think, "I'd rather not do the right thing today," we still *will* do the right thing, because we love what we have.

Here's the other thing that's important to remember: if it's just the structure and regimen of your life keeping you on the straight and narrow, then as soon as you lose the structure and regimen, you're going to lose control. You cannot rely on structure and regimen, because things happen. One day, you're going to forget to make your bed. Someone in your life will get sick. You'll have to travel. You will break your leg, or lose a job, or win the lottery. A million things can happen that will knock you off your regimen. But if you know who you are and have truly replaced that idealized version of yourself at the center of your life with a relationship with God, then it doesn't matter what life throws at you. You will remain steadfast.

As I've always said, to quit and quit for good, it's an inside job. It's God's business.

* * *

It is my hope that this book has helped you to understand in a practical, personal, and plainly stated way what the steps can do for you. Again, this book is not

To quit and quit for good, it's an inside job. It's God's business.

intended to replace the 12 Steps or a recovery program, but it can serve as an umbrella under which recovery can occur. It's a shape that will help you approach each step in your own time, when you are ready, while also living the rules and discipline of the 12 Steps immediately. This book has described what you'll be expected to do and the frame of mind you need to be in. This is a general guide to how you can incorporate these steps in your life, and an overview of what's coming.

I wrote this book as a way of reaching out to a person who is seeking help. Maybe you know someone like that. Maybe that person is you. Either way, this is a lifeline—a flashlight in the darkness. Reading it is likely just the first step of a long journey, and if you have found yourself reflected within these pages, it's time to find your community, find your program, and find the steps that are right for you.

Don't wait another minute to start saving your own life. Start today. Maybe it means getting into a program like ours, maybe it means finding a church you connect to, maybe it means beginning to attend meetings or finding a sponsor. Whatever it is, now is the moment to figure out what you're pairing this book with in order to take the next step toward a healthier, fuller life.

ABOUT THE AUTHOR

R everend Charles F. Plauché is the Senior Pastor of Haven House Mission Church. Victorious over addiction himself, Pastor Charles has dedicated his life to working with the chemically addicted. As Founder of Haven House Addiction Recovery in Santa Rosa Beach, Florida, Pastor Charles has developed a unique "handmade" program of recovery based on three basic Christian principles: rescue, restore, rebuild. For over twenty years, Pastor Charles's unique teaching ability has led many to the light of a new life. And twenty years later, Pastor Charles is still guiding staff members to excellence and working one-on-one with students to find freedom from bondage.

Haven House Addiction Recovery